Political Support in a Frustrated America

Political Support in a
Frustrated America

Stephen J. Farnsworth

Westport, Connecticut
London

Library of Congress Cataloging-in-Publication Data

Farnsworth, Stephen J., 1961–
    Political support in a frustrated America / Stephen J. Farnsworth.
        p. cm.
    Includes bibliographical references and index.
    ISBN 0–275–97729–3 (alk. paper)
    1. Political participation—United States. 2. Political culture—United States.
3. Legitimacy of governments—United States. 4. United States—Politics and
government—2001– 5. Political leadership—United States—Public opinion.
6. Public opinion—United States. I. Title.
JK1764.F37 2003
320.973—dc21   2003051052

British Library Cataloguing in Publication Data is available.

Library of Congress Catalog Card Number: 2003051052
ISBN: 0–275–97729–3

First published in 2003

Praeger Publishers, 88 Post Road West, Westport, CT 06881
An imprint of Greenwood Publishing Group, Inc.
www.praeger.com

Printed in the United States of America

The paper used in this book complies with the
Permanent Paper Standard issued by the National
Information Standards Organization (Z39.48–1984).

10 9 8 7 6 5 4 3 2 1

Contents

Tables

Acknowledgments

This project is the result of support generously offered from many sources. The first debt of course is to those who made their surveys available for the various versions of this study: the American National Elections Studies and the Congressional Perceptions poll provided by John Hibbing and Elizabeth Theiss-Morse. Thanks are also due to my twenty interviewees, who graciously discussed their deepest feelings about government with a complete stranger, and to Praeger's Michael Hermann, and Arlene Belzer and Alicia Lutz from Coastal Editorial Services.

I also wish to express my appreciation to my professors and fellow graduate students at Georgetown University and to my colleagues at Mary Washington College for having created stimulating environments in which to study and debate the nature of citizen attachments to government. In particular, I would like to thank James Lengle, Jack Dennis, Jack Kramer, Lew Fickett and Wesley Joe for their advice and support.

Above all, I am greatly indebted to Diana Owen, without whose encouragement, insight, creativity and extraordinary patience this work would not have been possible. She has read this project over and over again as it has developed over the last several years and has been an amazing teacher, mentor and friend.

Thanks are also are due for the many years of encouragement I have received from my parents and from Tanya DeKona, who in particular has endured much grief as the companion of an anxious graduate student and equally anxious assistant professor these last several years.

Early parts of this research have been published elsewhere, and I thankfully acknowledge permission to reprint and refine the arguments previously presented in the following articles: "Federal Frustration, State Satisfaction? Voters and Decentralized Government Power," *Publius: The*

Journal of Federalism 29(3) (summer 1999): 75–88; "Citizen Evaluations of the Federal Government," *Virginia Social Science Journal* 38 (2003): 1–16; "Competing Citizen Views of Trust: Virginia Interviews on the Forms of Political and Personal Trust," *Virginia Social Science Journal* 36 (winter 2001): 43–59; "Political Support and Citizen Frustration: Testing Three Linkage Theories," *Virginia Social Science Journal* 35 (2000): 69–84; "Loving and Loathing Virginia: Feelings about Federalism in the Old Dominion," *Virginia Social Science Journal* 34 (1999): 15–38. These articles were particularly useful in the development of the material presented in chapters 5 and 6.

All conclusions in this work, as well as any errors or omissions, are my responsibility.

1

A Crisis of Discontent and Alienation?

INTRODUCTION

What do Americans want from our government? It depends on whom you ask.

The ballots that could be counted promptly from the 2000 elections indicate that 51 million people wanted Vice President Al Gore to be president and 50.5 million people wanted Texas Governor George W. Bush to be president. Looking at the states, as the Constitution dictates that we must, a plurality of voters in thirty states (including Florida, which was settled by a U.S. Supreme Court decision) with 271 electoral votes said Bush should be president, compared to voters in twenty states and the District of Columbia with 267 electoral votes who favored Gore. (Gore received only 266 electoral votes though, as one Washington, D.C., elector left her ballot blank to draw attention to the cause of D.C. statehood.)

The deeply divided country looked the same from the other end of Pennsylvania Avenue. Voters who went to the polls on November 8, 2000, chose to be represented by fifty Democratic senators and fifty Republican ones and by a House of Representatives where Republicans won a very slim majority.

Or, if you were to look at the 2000 elections another way, you might note that only 51 percent of those eligible to do so cast a vote for president. Roughly 100.4 million people, about the same number of citizens who voted for Bush and Gore combined, stayed home for the closest presidential election in more than a century, according to the Committee for the Study of the American Electorate.

If you look at the national government in yet another way, you can see that Americans do not always get what they want from Congress.

Americans, by a margin of roughly two to one, tell pollsters that Congress should pass term-limits legislation. By roughly the same margin, citizens opposed the House decision to impeach President Bill Clinton over the Lewinsky matter. The Senate, the branch designed to be *less* directly tied to public opinion, did what a majority of citizens wanted and acquitted the president.

Despite these disagreements, voters returned to the Congress in 1998 and 2000 nearly every incumbent lawmaker seeking another term, regardless of whether they defied the public's will on term limits, dragged their feet on plans to enact campaign finance reform or voted for Clinton's impeachment. Even members who opposed the public on all three issues were returned, often by comfortable margins.

So, in the wake of what Comedy Central's *The Daily Show* called "Indecision 2000," voters remain steamed. Only one-third of citizens told pollsters that year that politicians could be trusted to do the right thing most or all of the time, and roughly three-quarters said that the federal government was run more for the benefit of a few big interests than for ordinary citizens.

Less than a year after that contentious election, on September 11, 2001, the United States was attacked by terrorists and suffered the greatest one-day loss of life since the Japanese attack on Pearl Harbor, Hawaii, on December 7, 1941. The attack brought about a renewed patriotism among many citizens and triggered an unusually long period of extremely high public approval ratings for the commander in chief, causing some to wonder whether citizen discontent with government might disappear for an extended period. But this was not to be. Within a year of September 11, 2001, the bursting of the tech-investment "bubble" and the apparent fraud practiced by major American corporations like Enron, Arthur Andersen and WorldCom, helped create new demons in the public's estimation: crooked CEOs and the government officials who have protected them. Flags adorning houses and cars notwithstanding, public opinion regarding the national government had shown clear signs of returning to where it was before the terrorist attacks: profoundly skeptical concerning governmental performance (Booth 2002; Kohut 2002; Stevenson and Elder 2002). Within months of the destruction of the World Trade Center in New York, Bin Laden was replaced by the economy as the voters' top concern (Kohut 2002).

This renewed citizen frustration with government, though it dissipated briefly in the weeks after the 2001 terrorist attacks, had been building for years before that attack. Measures of overall public confidence and trust in government had fallen dramatically from the levels of the mid-1960s and ever since has shown few signs of rebounding in any permanent way. Self-proclaimed political outsiders promising to shake things up—be they Bill Clinton, Ross Perot, Newt Gingrich or Pat Buchanan—gain public attention and public support, at least for a while (Barta 1993; Dennis and Owen 1994; Owen and Dennis 1996). But before long, they too become enveloped in the pervasive fog of distrust, cynicism and contempt that surrounds the public image of government generally and of Washington in particular (Citrin 1996; Craig 1996; Greider 1992). President Bill Clinton, who enjoyed high public approval ratings throughout much of his second term, found that even his supporters had grave doubts about his honesty and character (Cronin and Genovese 1998). Among his enemies, Clinton generated and continues to generate—even as a former president—an extraordinarily intense contempt, a force widespread enough and powerful enough to lead to years of taxpayer-financed investigations into Clinton's conduct as governor and as president and the failed attempt to drive Clinton from the White House in the late 1990s. Bush's high approval ratings of mid-2002, coupled with high levels of citizen frustration with government generally, show much the same disconnect between a generally popular president and the poorly regarded government seen during Clinton's second term (Booth 2002).

Voter anger over the imperfect method of counting the votes in Election 2000—the most contentious presidential election in more than a century—is only a recent example of how the public's current discontent and frustration represents more than an ordinary skepticism about this country's political leaders. (Halfway into Bush's first term, bumper stickers proclaiming "Re-elect Gore" began to make their appearance in Washington.) In the decade before that contentious election, a many researchers found that Americans were highly critical of the existing system of politics and government itself (Citrin 1996; Harwood Group 1991; Hibbing and Theiss-Morse 1995; Matthews 1994). Such citizens often supported campaign finance reform or proposed constitutional amendments that would require term limits or a balanced budget to restrain further our elected officials (Cronin 1989; Magleby 1984). Some supported even greater change—such things as electronic town meetings and picking legislators through lotteries—in the belief that the citizens themselves could do a far better job of running this country than the people doing so now (Becker 1993; Davis and Owen 1998; Georges 1993; Owen and Farnsworth 1995).

This desire for changing current political practice also has been seen through the growing interest in reempowering state government (Derthick 1987; Farnsworth 1999a, 1999b). This revived "power to the states" proposal has been offered as a means of bringing at least some governmental functions closer to home, where such actions might be better subject to public scrutiny and more efficiently administered than governmental functions controlled by far-off Washington. (In many states, voters have initiative and referendum powers to keep state governments in check.) People of varying ideological hues have been willing to consider favorably the idea of giving more power to state governments (cf., Gingrich 1995; Nathan 1990; Rivlin 1992). Even former President Clinton, for eight years the head of the party defined largely by its expansion of the federal government's scope, sought to increase his appeal to voters in 1996 by handing more responsibility for welfare policy to the states (Keeter 1997; Nelson 1997). George W. Bush promised during the 2000 presidential campaign to tip the balance more in favor of state governments and tried to do so during the early part of his term, at least until September 11, 2001.

A few citizens, of course, have gone further than most in giving vent to their objections to the current American system of politics and government. While their numbers are small, some people have done all they can either to isolate themselves from this nation or to strike out against it—as Waco, Oklahoma City, the Militia movement, the Unabomber, the so-called American Taliban, Ruby Ridge, the Montana Freemen and the self-proclaimed (and short-lived) Republic of Texas demonstrate, all too often with tragic results.

WHAT ARE THE SOURCES OF CITIZEN FRUSTRATION?

Few citizens would express any enthusiasm for political terrorists like those discussed above. But large numbers of citizens have said in poll after poll that the national government in Washington is falling short in a number of areas, including spending taxpayer money responsibly, representing the interests of ordinary citizens, and generally behaving in a trustworthy manner. Depending on the type of question asked, the frustration can be quite widespread. Fewer than one in five citizens believes that the national government pays "a good deal" of attention to what ordinary citizens want when the government makes policy, and three out of every five citizens believe that government wastes "a lot" of taxpayer money.

Researchers who have examined citizen frustration and its consequences for governance sometimes question whether advanced Western societies are up to the task of satisfying a sufficient level of demands from an energized and critical citizenry to enable these societies to thrive or, failing that, to survive. In other words, it is certainly not easy for government to keep voters happy, especially as the public's policy demands keep expanding into more controversial areas and as the challenges faced by government extend into more difficult areas like fighting international terrorism.

This first theory, one of "demand overload," is popular with many researchers. Ronald Inglehart (1977, 1981, 1988, 1990), for example, argued that growing numbers of voters in these modern democracies are

bigger and greater demands

seeking far more meaning from the political world than was the case previously, when a political system's ability to deliver a generally healthy economy basically could secure sufficient support for a given political order. The relative satisfaction of basic wants in these societies has led to a vast array of new demands upon government, particularly with respect to quality of life issues like the environment and the welfare state, where government may not be as capable of managing a society's progress. Under this perspective, citizens are thought to ask government to focus not on the areas where it has the most experience and where there is the most public consensus (just about everyone prefers a strong economy to a weak one), but to concentrate on far more contentious matters, like economic redistribution policies.

These newer demands often do not lend themselves to any clear consensus regarding the appropriate ends and means. How much pollution is acceptable when balanced against costs of public health, Superfund cleanups and lost jobs? How can government best secure the opportunity for individuals to maximize their potential as human beings? Should government help build a sense of belonging among its citizens—and, if so, how? These are, of course, far more difficult matters for people to consider and reach consensus on than is whether to keep the economy functioning smoothly. These are likewise far more difficult matters for government to manage, even if a general public consensus emerges on what should be done.

The Inglehart model suggests that political support has become much more difficult for individuals to give and much more difficult for nations to get in the modern context. The protestant asceticism that helped build much of Western capitalist society once led to few public demands upon national governments. As recently as World War II, citizens in the United States endured relatively great sacrifices—including what for this country represented heavy military casualties and severe economic privation—to defeat Hitler. Likewise, the depression was a time of great forbearance for many of today's more elderly citizens. Recent demands upon government, in contrast, are all over the lot—and sometimes even are contradictory. Besides the basic desire for fulfillment in life (something that would have struck many previous generations as an unimaginable luxury), contemporary policy demands of government include such areas as environmentalism, participatory democracy, women's rights, pacifist issues, arms reduction and the promotion and development of renewable energy sources.

Jurgen Habermas (1973:50) also thought today's citizens may be "overloading" Western political systems through new and more complicated needs. Examples of these factors in the American context include the growing controversies surrounding governmental policies such as affirmative action, environmental regulation and the nation's long-term debt.

The debt in turn is tied directly to federal funding for programs such as welfare, environmental protection, health care and Social Security. The federal government's assistance programs replaced the cultural tradition of the needy being the responsibility of their families, their churches or, in the last resort, their local communities. When governments are asked to perform outside of traditional areas of responsibility and competence, governments face tougher standards against which a given country's performance will be judged by citizens.

In the past, economic downturns were seen as a more natural part of the rhythm of life. Now many citizens believe that any subpar economic performance is the state's fault, according to Habermas. The frustration stemming from these economic shortcomings may be particularly pronounced among younger Americans raised during the economic booms of recent decades, which are so far from the recessionary 1970s, much less the Great Depression (Howe and Strauss 1993). While the late 1990s were marked by relatively good times, many youthful dot-com millionaires became ex-millionaires following a series of stock market declines in 2000, 2001 and 2002.

Where patriotism once sufficed to secure public loyalty, massive income flows into government coffers are now required, and the subsequent state-sponsored distribution and redistribution is clearly a more cumbersome and divisive process for any nation. Individuals who once might have taken problems of poverty more into their own hands by virtue of necessity now have the option of simply waiting for a state's welfare payments, job retraining and other assistance programs. Even the rise of patriotism that occurred in the wake of September 11, 2001, as of this writing, does not appear to have generated any long-term realignment in citizen general orientations toward government. If anything, the range of demands upon government have expanded even further following the terrorist attacks. The "demand overload" problem may therefore be even greater now than it was a decade ago.

One does not need to be a free-market conservative to note the widespread governmental intervention in economic matters far removed from overall national economic policy. Wages for all sorts of jobs are set at least partially by government policy in concert with market forces, be it through such things as minimum wage laws, restrictions on hours and conditions or through vocational training, trade policies, government contracts and economic development incentives for certain regions and particular industries (Offe 1984). Workers, companies and government are all involved, but conditions are more complicated than any three-way jostling for advantage. Even when the interests of management, labor and government can be balanced, there is still room for disagreement. There can be no assurances, after all, that interests of those outside the union and management spheres—say, supporters of women's rights and environmentalists—will not push also to be included in the debate (Held 1987:218–19). No matter what a modern democratic government does—even if it does nothing—political leaders can make new enemies, and plenty of them at that, in today's demand-laden political environment.

Politicians are elected to do the public's bidding, and the public shows no signs of reducing the volume of demands upon government anytime soon, particularly in America. Consider what politicians hear from constituents: Build this bridge and highway; keep pharmaceutical prices down; keep floodwaters away; make sure there is a lot of affordable heating oil, gasoline and electricity around; watch to be certain that there are plenty of jobs; keep foods and medicines and communities safe; take the trash away; educate the children; keep the terrorists away; make sure my stock market investments do not lose value and, while you are it, lower my taxes.

The fact that no governmental system would be capable of satisfying these complex, if not conflicting, demands may be beside the point. These are the strict standards against which a modern Western government is judged. Falling short—and a government often does—can lead to a growing and general frustration with a political regime, regardless of the particular demand or demands sought by a given individual. Today's demand-filled political environment gives a citizen a generous buffet of policy shortcomings from which to select the source or sources of one's own discontent. To make matters worse from the perspective of government officials, increased citizen education leads to increased citizen sophistication. This in turn can lead to harsher evaluations of government performance and a greater willingness to voice complaints (Rosenau 1988).

Clearly, the idea that government is asked to do too much resonates in today's economically lumbering and politically shrill environment. Indeed, one might note that the harshest political battles of recent years in this country have been over the government's relatively new social welfare responsibilities, including health care, welfare and the environment (Mann and Ornstein 1995; Rushefsky 1996; Skocpol 1997; Vig and Kraft 2003).

A second theory that seeks to link citizen frustration to political support focuses on the processes of government rather than the outcomes. This approach is quite familiar to people who were paying attention to the campaign finance reform debates in Congress during recent years and during the 2000 Republican presidential nomination campaign. It therefore will need less explanation. This second perspective, dubbed "procedural frustration," holds that citizens are troubled by unfair governmental processes at least as much as they are by the actions actually undertaken by government (Tyler 1988; Tyler and Rasinski 1991). In

other words, people may be angrier about feeling shut out of government policy-making than about the actual decisions government officials
make. This approach just might be called simply, the "McCain campaign" perspective. U.S. Senator John McCain (R-Ariz.), after all, sought
the Republican Party's nomination for president in 2000 largely on the
basis of promising to curb special interest influence in Washington and
to make the views of ordinary citizens more prominent in Washington.
McCain generated a great deal of public enthusiasm for his candidacy,
but he eventually lost the nomination to then–Texas Governor George
W. Bush, who spent roughly $70 million (much of it in special interest
money) to defeat the senator. During the 107th Congress, which began
in January 2001, McCain quickly returned to promoting his plans for
campaign finance reform on Capitol Hill, and the measure was signed
reluctantly by President Bush in 2002 (Drew 2002).

Perhaps the most prominent academic examination of this second perspective is found in the work of John R. Hibbing and Elizabeth Theiss-
Morse, the authors of *Congress as Public Enemy* (1995). They maintained
that citizens are particularly troubled by the inefficiency, the bickering
and the insider-oriented natures of legislating in America.

Anger and frustration may be common emotional reactions for many
citizens thinking about government outcomes and procedures, but apathy and resignation are also common responses. An alternative to the
"demand overload" and "procedural frustrations" theses is the belief
that frustrated citizens may be "tuning out." Drawing on his empirical
study of the civic traditions in Italy, Robert D. Putnam (1973, 1993a,
1993b, 1993c, 1995a, 1995b, 2000) suggested a third point of view: Declines in American political participation stem in part from the decline
of the "civic community," a basic faith or trust in one's community and
in one's fellow citizens. This "social trust" is a distinct concept from the
"political trust" that relates to how one feels about political authorities.
This "tuning out" thesis is also known as "bowling alone" in recognition
of Putnam's work on this question.

What is different about this third perspective, of course, is Putnam's
emphasis—he focused not on an individual's direct relationship with
government but rather on one's interrelationship with other citizens. But
the three perspectives clearly are interrelated in that one's political in-
volvements with fellow citizens are an important part of one's perspective regarding the political system's procedures and outcomes,
particularly in democratic nations like the United States. Further, cynicism about or hostility toward people would not likely be suspended
when a citizen approaches a government that, after all, is comprised of
fellow human beings. In fact, if surveys are any guide, public cynicism
about people may be intensified when one considers individuals in government as officials rather than just fellow citizens. This increased hos-

tility may be particularly strong for government officials held in particularly low regard, most notably members of Congress (Dodd 1993; Hibbing and Theiss-Morse 1995).

WHAT ARE THE CONSEQUENCES OF DISCONTENT?

The key question in a consideration of political support in America is stated simply: Just how deep is the American "reservoir" of goodwill toward its political system? Other than perhaps in some of the minds of the radicals of the 1960s, the equally simple answer traditionally had been the rather vague, "deep enough." Paul Sniderman (1981) found no politically significant alternative plans for government in the United States that were being taken seriously, even in relatively alternative northern California. He found very few people wanted to abandon America. Many of the most-alienated citizens wanted to stay, and the very, very few people surveyed who did express a willingness to go somewhere else said they favored moving to countries that they envisioned as very similar to America, advanced Western capitalist democracies like Australia or Canada (Sniderman 1981:130).

The lack of an alternative structure in the minds of many citizens is a key factor leading to greater system stability in the United States, according to Sniderman.

Even among the disaffected who openly called for a change in the system of government there was no intelligible trace of an alternative political vocabulary, of an alternative political order. (Sniderman 1981:151)

Although American culture is in many aspects diverse, it is in one aspect unvarying: it neither conceives nor harbors competitive conceptions of the political order. (Sniderman 1981:168)

America's tradition of expressing considerable criticism of political leaders and political structures is also very healthy, Sniderman said. "Those who are overready to approve of government are overready to yield to it," Sniderman (1981:148) wrote.

Samuel P. Huntington (1981) suggested that American politics suffers from a persistent gap between political ideals and the inability of political institutions to live up to those admittedly exacting standards. Huntington argued that the widespread American belief that strong government is oppressive and therefore illegitimate helps explain why American government is not necessarily as efficient as other political systems—and suggests that the American people do not really want all that much efficiency in their government.

In the American context there will always be those who say that the institutional glass is half-empty and who will spill much passion attempting to fill it to the brim from the spring of idealism. But in the nature of things, particularly in America, it can never be much more than half-full. (Huntington 1981:12)

The state of political support in this country could be worse, of course. The vast majority of citizens at least quietly accept the political and governmental system and vote (or passively abstain), pay their taxes and otherwise function as loyal—or, at worst, as indifferent—citizens. Most people, even many of the harsher critics of today's government and politics, consider themselves patriotic. A generation ago, when many automobile bumpers offered the maxim, "America: Love It or Leave It," few favored the latter option (Sniderman 1981). Indeed, some of the most alienated Americans of the 1960s stayed here and tried to promote racial equality and an end to the Vietnam War from within, through peaceful demonstrations, court challenges and political campaigns and elections (Jennings and Niemi 1968, 1974, 1981). The same is true today. For all the public discontent, America remains one of the world's few nations never to have had a period of substantial emigration.

Indeed, this contrasting argument that America is not undergoing severe strain rests in many ways on such an international comparison. National political and governmental systems come and go, and that has never been so clear as in the past two decades, when a variety of regimes in Eastern Europe, Asia, Latin America and Africa have fallen and nations have begun to build new political systems (cf., Dahl 1992; Poggi 1990). America may have its racial problems, but it does not have the system of apartheid that in recent years forced a new political system in South Africa. The American economy sometimes struggles, but it works dramatically better than the centrally planned and corrupt economies of the former Soviet Union and Eastern Europe or their successors (cf., Krickus 1987; Mason 1995). Nor does America have the dictatorial one-party or one-person rule that led to unrest in the Philippines under Ferdinand Marcos, the Soviet Union and in nations across Eastern Europe, the Middle East and Latin America (Gottlieb 1993).

What ferment we do have in America today, this line of thinking goes, is a sign of the strength of the political and governmental system, not a manifestation of its weakness. People do not have to rise up violently to demand change; they can make their arguments and organize. All have a chance to prevail peacefully, at least in theory. The number of people supporting changes within the political system rather than outside it suggests that members of the mass public widely accept the view that peaceful change can best be accomplished through within–system activism (Craig and Wald 1985).

The scholars who tend to be less troubled by citizen discontent argue that the American political and governmental system is not supposed to purr with the fine hum of a well-oiled machine, rather, it is supposed to be a lumbering, somewhat inefficient contraption. In fact, public tensions can be quite useful, for they keep government from becoming too oppressive. The Framers of the U.S. Constitution, after all, advised that some public frustration with outcomes and procedures was a small price to pay for avoiding the despotism that may come from a highly responsive and efficient system.

But this line of argument, expressed early on and most clearly in *The Federalist*, does not conclude that citizen discontent is unimportant (Hamilton, Madison and Jay 1990 [1787–88]). Rather, the Framers believed that the system they developed could respond to public pressures before conditions reached a boiling point, that is, before the system underwent any crisis that threatened its legitimacy or its survival. In short, some public discontent may be good because it may keep politicians somewhat honest, but too much discontent clearly can have serious negative consequences.

Americans may be frustrated, and frustration may lead to change, but frustration at current levels does not seem all that likely to lead to revolutionary change. A radical restructuring of America along even twentieth century European lines is simply beyond the experience of anyone who has spent his or her life in the United States, and, indeed, may be almost beyond our collective imagination (Sniderman 1981). But the grave public discontent that ultimately can lead to regime instability is steadily growing more familiar to Americans and recently has attracted the renewed interest of researchers (cf., Craig 1996; Hibbing and Theiss-Morse 1995). In other words, the question is not simply a matter of whether the existing political system can survive—few scholars of any ideology are predicting any immediate disintegration of today's political structure—rather, it is one of the relative health of the U.S. political system.

> Though [stable advanced states] are unlikely to be threatened with revolution, there is a great and visible difference between the situations confronting the government in a polity whose citizens are suspicious about leaders' motives and doubtful of their competence, and that confronting a government whose citizens assume that their institutions and governors typically produce fair and effective policies. (Weatherford 1987:6)

The conviction that government no longer works has been growing for some time and is not likely to dissipate soon. Out of these bone-

deep frustrations immense pressures for change are building. (Yankelovich 1991:4–5)

It is difficult to know exactly what might be done to keep the confidence gap from becoming a permanent feature of the American
political landscape. None of the "reforms" either enacted or proposed in recent years—e.g., limits on the number of terms that
elected officials can serve, imposing tax ceilings on state legislatures
(or passing a balanced budget amendment to the U.S. Constitution),
prohibiting Congress from awarding itself an immediate pay raise
(the Twenty Seventh Amendment), making wider use of initiative
and referendum elections, changing state and federal campaign finance laws (public funding, spending caps, eliminating PACs [po-
litical action committees], free television time for candidates or
parties), requiring strict financial disclosure from individuals who
hold key government positions, using independent prosecutors to
pursue wrongdoers etc.—are apt to have a huge effect, though
some may serve the symbolic purpose of supplying an outlet for
the disaffected to vent their anger at politicians who are seen as
being remote and inaccessible. (Craig 1996:63)

Our own constitutional history, starting with the Bill of Rights, stresses
the importance of establishing a flexible political system, one able to
change and to bend, at least somewhat, to address new needs and conditions. The U.S. political system may not work with the efficiency imag-
ined by some of the world's would-be social engineers, but this nation's
capacity to change creates a means of at least mitigating public frustrations with the status quo without having to create a new American republic. This is probably the most important consequence of high levels
of discontent. Declining citizen support for government is likely to make
government more rigid, as citizens under all but the most extraordinary
circumstances are likely to have too little trust in their elected officials
to give them the latitude to deal effectively with future problems and
needs. Regardless of whether the problem of discontent involves procedural frustration, a demand overload or a breakdown of community,
continuing discontent weakens the ties between and among the individuals who—through their votes and through their other forms of participation in politics and government—give direction to elected officials
and help shape public policies (Kushma 1988; Lazare 1996; Tocqueville
1960 [1835]).

To some, the question is actually how much mitigating this somewhat
cumbersome political system can provide. Some writers argued that it is
just this resistance to governmental modifications that has triggered the
declining level of public confidence in the current political system. A few

special interests that have captured the attentions of key legislators are able to stymie public policies favored by large majorities of the American public and are driving people to ever-greater frustrations, according to some critics of the status quo.

> Since meaningful representation is impossible, a typical citizen has three choices. He can give up and tune out in front of the TV set. He can vote with his feet by moving to a jurisdiction where the public amenities are better and the taxes lower. Or, if he can't move but still doesn't like how things around him are shaping up, he can go on the warpath against government in general. The first means retreating into the privacy of one's own home, the second means turning oneself into a consumer of government services rather than a citizen, while the third means joining up in one of the mindless populist revolts that have been contorting the American landscape ever since Proposition 13. Unfortunately none of them works. (Lazare 1996:257)

To Daniel Lazare, then, the constitutional system represents a dangerous reverence for the past, applying somewhat carelessly the philosophies of the eighteenth century to the difficulties of modernity. The nation's current problems require substantial structural change, in his view.

> Americans must stop thinking of democracy as a legacy of the Founders and a gift of the Gods, something that allows millions of voters to cry "Me! Me! Me!" while politicians and judges divide up the spoils according to some time-honored formula. Rather, they will have to think of it as an intellectual framework that they create and continuously update, one that allows them to tackle the problems of the modern world, not as individuals, but as a society. If democracy is to survive, it must grow. And if it is to grow, it must detach itself from the pre-democratic 18th century norms and take its place in the modern world. (Lazare 1996:299)

Even if one accepts the argument that government should be redesigned, or at least modified, in response to citizen discontent, there are a number of possible approaches. Ross Perot, who ran for president as a third-party candidate in 1992 and 1996, proposed "electronic town meetings" more than a decade ago, and a number of political scientists, including President Woodrow Wilson, have long urged that America develop a stronger system of political parties comparable to those found in Western Europe. Still another option is found in the devolution movement, which holds that the national government in Washington should hand many of its responsibilities off to state and local governments. While there is no consensus on which of these alternatives might solve which problems, the vigorous debate and considerable citizen discontent with government demonstrates that the American political system has been undergoing a period of unusual ferment lately, one worthy of further consideration.

HOW DOES ONE INVESTIGATE POLITICAL SUPPORT?

To evaluate these competing perspectives, one needs to consider broad trends regarding public opinion about the national government and pay special attention to how citizen feelings have changed in recent years. Where has trust in government declined? How has the perception of governmental competence changed? How do people view the federal government when compared to state and local governmental authorities?

One also must consider matters of context. What are the causes of increased cynicism—the declining performance of government, perhaps, or perhaps the increasingly negative presentation of those conditions by the media? Are people more cynical because politicians are more incompetent and/or more corrupt than they used to be? Are the problems faced by this nation today harder to solve than those in the past? Have we lost faith in each other as fellow citizens?

Who exactly are the most discontented: Are they younger citizens or, perhaps, the older ones? Are the heaviest media users those with the most negative opinions concerning government and politics?

The final issues in considering political support are whether leaders and/or citizens should care about this growing public discontent and what, if anything, should citizens and government do to alleviate these frustrations?

This somewhat daunting list of questions will be addressed in the chapters that follow. The next step in this chapter is to think more about the types of public support for government. The discussion then turns to federalism and discusses how greater power for state governments may represent a useful response to citizen discontent focused on Washington. This chapter then concludes with an outline of what will be covered in subsequent chapters.

RETURNING TO POLITICAL SUPPORT

For those who study politics, the debate over how changes in political support for the government and for governmental factors may affect the health of a political regime has been going on for quite some time. Ancient Greek philosophers, particularly Plato and Aristotle, considered how to construct a government system likely to obtain widespread public support, or at least widespread public acceptance. Some of their ideas, as well as those of Thomas Hobbes, John Locke, Jean-Jacques Rousseau and others, were applied to the American system by America's own Founding Fathers, three of whom discussed the issue of public support for government at length in *The Federalist* (Hamilton, Madison and Jay 1990 [1787–88]), the most significant early explanation of the Constitution.

Compared to other countries, the United States has had comparatively great support for the traditional constitutional order and the political institutions organized in 1787 and operating without interruption for more than two centuries. As many older countries have gone through monarchies, despots, democracy, convulsive geographic expansions and contractions and countless changes in regime structures, the U.S. system has remained largely constant. What change has occurred, excluding the unique and temporary circumstances of the Civil War period, generally has involved little more than tinkering in the margins of the political system and a steady expansion westward (Turner 1962). American government modifications that have occurred, such as changes in voting laws and the direct election of senators, have little in common with the magnitude of change represented by the shifts from one form of government to another in France, the anti-czar and anti-Soviet revolutions in Russia or the movements toward and away from monarchy-oriented systems in many European countries.

But America still has had its rough patches, historically speaking. In the 1960s, when the United States endured internal ferment brought on primarily by segregation and by the Vietnam War, U.S. scholars began to focus with a new intensity on the nature of mass public loyalty to the U.S. political system. The central paradigm for studying citizen views concerning government then—and now—has two dimensions. Scholars such as David Easton and Jack Dennis argued that citizens have a fundamental emotional attachment to the political system, an attachment that binds a citizen to his or her country very strongly. They call this first type of citizen orientation "diffuse support." Easton and Dennis also argue that there is a second type of citizen orientation to government, one that relates much more directly to explicit evaluations of governmental performance. They call this form of citizen evaluation "specific support." The emotional attachment, which is the most important for measuring the public support for a political system, is largely separate from what the political system does for an individual in any specific way.

> By diffuse support we mean the generalized trust and confidence that members invest in various objects of the (political) system as ends in themselves. The peculiar quality of this kind of attachment to an object is that it is not contingent on any quid pro quo; it is

offered unconditionally. In its extreme form it may appear as blind loyalty or unshakable patriotism. (Easton and Dennis 1969:62–63)

Diffuse support, then, is the "reservoir" of general goodwill held by the citizenry toward their own political system. It is the glue that more or less holds America together. This profound emotional attachment to one's government helps the political system survive crises like depressions and wars. It also enables government officials to convince many citizens to undergo inconvenient and sometimes dangerous personal hardships, ranging from paying taxes to military service, for the sake of maintaining or advancing their political system (Easton and Dennis 1969: 62–64). Without this fundamental support, individuals and groups might ignore and perhaps turn against a system that consistently frustrates them.

In other words, diffuse support can be defined broadly as the general emotional attachment to a citizen's political system. This attachment is contingent not on particular policies and leaders, but rather on one's perspective on the institutions of government itself. Diffuse support is roughly analogous to faith in a nation, a long-term and not easily shaken belief in a set of political institutions (Easton 1975).

Easton and Dennis (1969:62–63) saw diffuse support as encompassing at least patriotism and trust. The portrait of the concept was drawn in contrasts, with specific support representing the antithesis. Specific support, which relates to how one feels about individual politicians and particular policies, clearly is tied to the intellectual assessment of specific matters rather than to the broad sweep of emotional perspectives citizens have about a political system. Specific support is the "quid pro quo" dimension of political support. In this dichotomous formulation, diffuse support is largely separate from the particulars of the here and now that affect specific support (Easton 1975).

While the Easton and Dennis model has been very controversial, their model (or a closely linked derivative of it) occupies a central place for those considering the stability and the long-term health of a political regime (cf., Craig 1993, 1996; Hibbing and Theiss-Morse 1995; Parker 1986; Sears et al. 1978; Stewart 1986; Wright 1976). This study considers political support through a variety of measures, including democratic satisfaction and evaluations of the political system and its components. These measures correspond to the general approaches in political science used to study political support, be it defined as diffuse and specific support or some similar concept.

More than three decades ago, Vietnam, civil rights and the Watergate scandal provided obvious and dramatic referents for shaping how people felt about their political system (Jennings and Niemi 1968, 1974, 1981). While the current political environment seems to lack such powerful and divisive circumstances, the steady demoralizing recounting of shortcomings in virtually all aspects of the current political world—presidents, legislators, the justice system and even the local public schools—also may trigger a corrosive effect on political support (Craig 1993, 1996; Dionne 1991; Greider 1992). This can be the case even though today's societal "malaise" is not tied to a single dramatic event of the magnitude of Vietnam or Watergate. The bitterly divided and intensely contested presidential election (and postelection) of 2000 does not seem to have been as influential on today's young people as the crises over Vietnam and Watergate were on earlier generations, if only because citizens of all ages were quite frustrated with the government before November 8, 2000. Perhaps the terrorist attacks of September 11, 2001, will be the politically formative event for today's young people, but the evidence so far suggests that less has changed regarding citizen frustration with government than one might have expected.

RETURNING TO FEDERALISM?

Surveys have shown that the vast majority of citizens consider the U.S. form of government the best on Earth (though they may not be all that ready to explain why, even when such a follow-up question is asked). Sniderman (1981) noted this comparison difficulty, that is, that people may not have much of an alternative conception of government in their minds.

But perhaps Sniderman and other past researchers did not pay enough attention to the most viable alternative model, one that would have been admittedly unpopular when memories of the segregated South were more recent. Perhaps this alternative model, enhanced power for state governments and less authority for Washington, simply has become more attractive with the passage of time. Regardless, the past decade has been marked by growing interest in or support for a revived federalism on the part of many politicians, citizens and even some academics (Connolly 1997; Donahue 1997; Farnsworth 1999a, 1999b; Hetherington and Nugent 1998; Lowi 1979; Nathan 1990; Rivlin 1992).

The enhanced state-power alternative is not so far-fetched as it might seem at first: Taking power from Washington and putting more of it in the hands of state and local officials has been an uneasy debate since the founding and has found renewed life of a sort in the Republican Party's "Contract with America" (Gingrich 1995) and in the Republican presidential campaigns of both Bob Dole in 1996 and George W. Bush in 2000. Some Democrats, including President Clinton, also have endorsed the concept. Giving more power to the state governments was a key part of the welfare reform legislation President Clinton signed in 1996 (Cammisa 1998). This alternative, therefore, should elicit in most citizens at least a spark of recognition, and with it the potential for a more meaningful comparative analysis involving the status quo. It is also an alternative consistent with the philosophy behind much of the sporadic violence against the national government: that power in the United States has become far too centralized and that subnational political authorities tend to be less illegitimate (Gugliotta 1995; Wood 1995).

While some might prefer to focus on another alternative political system, perhaps electronic democracy, such technologically advanced ideas still seem a bit too utopian and unknown among the mass public for widespread public discussion and evaluation. Some revival of the "power to the states" doctrine—albeit with a less racially oriented focus than was the case in the 1950s and 1960s—is far more a part of current mass political debate than an electronic version of the traditional town meeting, regardless of the eventual prospects for cyberdemocracy. Likewise, a political and governmental system more closely modeled on the idea of "responsible" political parties, like those party organizations found in the British Parliament, seems too far removed from this country's current political debates—and too explicitly foreign—to be an effective means of securing an objective evaluation of the strengths and weaknesses of our own status quo. This is true even though the responsible political parties idea has long been popular among political scientists (cf., Ranney 1962; Schattschneider 1977; Wilson 1908).

"Power to the states," therefore, is homegrown enough to be roughly as American as the Washington-dominant status quo, well known enough—particularly in some parts of the country—to serve as a comparison, but different enough to provide a useful contrast between what is and what might be. As such, it seems the best choice for an alternative sovereignty that can lead to an effective comparison with and evaluation of the status quo. The fact that most Americans view their state governments more positively than the national government offers yet another reason to pursue this comparative approach (Farnsworth 1999b).

AN OVERVIEW OF THE RESEARCH APPROACH

This investigation uses a variety of national surveys, and particularly recent American National Election Studies (ANES). Levels of support for the political system and the parts of the government are explained through a variety of independent variables. These measures cover such topics as whether an individual believes the government listens to him or her and whether he or she believes the political system operates in the public interest and is therefore deserving of trust. Other relevant topics relate to whether the system is thought to operate in a competent manner and is capable of keeping the economy on the right track.

The national surveys are essential for comparing changes in the public's emotional attachments to government over time. The ANES, in particular, is vital to a study of this nature because few national surveys provide as valuable a long-term collection of survey questions on the issue of mass support as they do. Many of the questions asked in the most recent surveys were part of the battery of questions asked at least every four years since the 1960s or, in some cases, even earlier.

An approach that relies solely on mass-survey research seems insufficient, in part because citizens do not think solely in multiple-choice responses. By their very nature, such survey questions do not encourage respondents to delve deeply into profound values like federalism, patriotism and one's trust in a political system. What do these limited responses about big interests and government waste really mean? How do we as Americans conceptualize political trust and interpersonal trust? How do we feel about the national government vis-à-vis our own states' government? Indeed, there is a growing recognition among scholars that survey questions tapping public feelings about government tell only part of the story and that one-on-one interviews or focus groups provide important supplemental information (Craig 1993; Hibbing and Theiss-Morse 1995; Tolchin 1999).

Clearly then, there are advantages to using more than one technique. In addition to the quantitative analysis conducted here, this study will also take advantage of one-on-one, in-person interviews conducted to elicit more information regarding public views of political support, federalism and other citizen orientations toward government in America (Farnsworth 1997, 1999a). The ordinary citizens quoted here are rather diverse in terms of background, but their responses are not presumed to be empirically generalizable to the population of this country or even of east-central Virginia, where the interviews were conducted. Even so, these somewhat open-ended conversations offer new insights into the study of political support, a concept that has had more than its share of developmental difficulties. These interviews, after all, suggest new and improved measures for a concept that is vital for understanding the long-term operations of a democratic society.

The interviewing part of the study allows this project to overcome a constant problem relating to public views about the U.S. political system and its effectiveness: the lack of a viable alternative political structure in the minds of nearly all U.S. citizens. Despite the intense frustration with government in the United States in recent decades, no clear alternative system—not parliamentary democracy, not dictatorship—commands any widespread recognition in this country, much less anything approaching even modest public acceptance (Sniderman 1981).

Both the ANES and the interviews can shed some light on this new alternative vision of a revived federalism. Questions asked in the ANES about citizens' relative feelings concerning the differing levels of government allow for an empirical test of the importance of enhanced state power as a way of explaining, understanding and perhaps reducing citizen discontent with Washington (Farnsworth 1999b). By asking the interviewees to consider the alternative of enhanced state power explicitly during the Virginia interviews, citizens can explore their own thoughts and feelings about what is specifically right and wrong with the system in existence now (Farnsworth 1999a).

WHAT COMES NEXT?

Following this introductory chapter, chapter 2 turns to a more detailed study of just how discontented Americans are and where that discontent is concentrated. Using surveys, this chapter examines political support through measures of general democratic satisfaction and evaluations of the overall political system. Starting in chapter 2 and continuing in the chapters that follow, this project will address the issue of how support may be linked to particular political experiences that have had special impacts on groups of citizens who came of age politically during specified periods. Examples of such influential events affecting long-term views toward government may include Vietnam, Watergate and World War II. Although more will be said on this point later, this study will use a four-generation framework developed by Strauss and Howe (1991): the Next generation (born 1961–1981), Baby Boomers (born 1943–1960), the Silent generation (born 1925–1942) and the G.I. generation (born 1901–1924).

Chapter 3 looks at political support as it relates to each of the three branches: Congress, the presidency and the judicial system. Each section of the chapter includes an assessment of overall findings and the important generational differences found in the political support relating to each branch of the political system. The same generational dividing lines are used throughout the project.

Chapter 4 looks at media usage and political support. The media represent key factors in learning about political events, particularly in the modern political environment (Cappella and Jamieson 1997; Iyengar and Kinder 1987; Cook 1998). Any study looking at public emotional attachments to politics must consider media's effects, since newspapers and particularly television have a good deal of influence over what an individual knows and how he or she generally relates to the political system (Cook 1998; Kerbel 1995). Many scholars have been highly critical of the mass media for generating, or at least exacerbating, the political cynicism and negativity thought to undermine Americans' faith in their political system (cf., Cappella and Jamieson 1997; Robinson 1976). Others condemn the media for generating excessive public cynicism through their focus on the trivial, like scandals and the horse-race aspects of political campaigns (Sabato 1993; Patterson 1993). Still others view the media as a sort of "great legitimator" in that the media focus on established authorities and keep nonmainstream figures out of the limelight (cf., Ginsberg 1986). This section of the study includes a consideration of how various types of media consumers vary in political support.

Chapter 5 moves beyond the traditional limited response format of mass survey research to use interviews to examine the political opinions of ordinary citizens in greater depth. In particular, the twenty people interviewed for this project were asked about political support generally as well as their assessments of the different levels of government (national, state and local). They were explicitly asked to assess a plan to give state government more powers and the national government less authority. A renewed federalism is a major alternative vision for the U.S. political order that is discussed frequently by politicians but one rarely examined in mass survey research. The twenty interviews in this project cannot be seen to represent national public opinion; indeed these Virginia respondents are likely to be far more pro-state than would interviewees who live outside the South. Nevertheless, considering their answers provides researchers with a theoretical richness not found in the traditional agree/neutral/disagree mass survey responses. The analysis of these expressed opinions permits more effective suggestions regarding the future direction of political support research.

In chapter 6, the focus turns to an evaluation of the state of political support, particularly its potential future trajectory. This chapter will offer further evidence regarding public assessments of the state governments— the closest thing to an alternative sovereignty in the American mind. It will also discuss the means for assessing the contents of the "reservoir" of political support and discussing its role in sustaining the U.S. system of government and politics. Central to this chapter are considerations of a renewed federalism, one possible way to adjust the American political structure.

2

"I Pledge Allegiance?": Support for the Political Regime

This chapter, which looks at the political system as a whole, begins by considering how citizen orientations toward government are established. We will consider how Americans feel about their national government and how those feelings have changed over time. We then examine generational differences in political experiences and how those differences manifest themselves in differing generational orientations toward the political system overall. In subsequent chapters we will look at public opinion concerning different parts of the political system, including Congress, the presidency, the judicial branch and the news media.

POLITICAL SOCIALIZATION: THE TIE THAT BINDS?

For four decades, David Easton (1953, 1965a, 1965b, 1975, 1976, 1990), Jack Dennis (1970, 1973, 1976, 1981)—both separately and together (Easton and Dennis 1967, 1969)—and many others have worked to develop answers to two key questions of political science (and of political life in general): How and why do political systems persist? These questions are hardly new—theorizing about the nature of the ideal state goes back at least to the ancient Greeks—but the difficulties in addressing these issues make them the perennials of political science.

Central to the survival of democratic political systems is public support for that political system. Wherever one looks at political systems and at the attempts to sustain them, one finds efforts to generate or intensify positive emotional feelings regarding one's country. Ancient Greeks and Romans told stories and performed pageants to commemorate the accomplishments of governments and governmental leaders. Centuries later the carefully tended legends of nationalist heroes like Joan of Arc and King Arthur helped bring together feudal and feuding principalities into what would become the modern nation-states of Europe. Even playwrights such as William Shakespeare did what they could to help build an English nationalist vision in their historical plays (King Henry V's speech to his army at Agincourt in Shakespeare's *Henry V* is an excellent example).

With the development of steadily more powerful governments and of increasingly comprehensive national media systems over the past century, efforts by the government to enhance public support for itself could be far more expansive than anything attempted by previous centuries, with their "bread and circuses" or their nationalistic theater. Films like *The Triumph of the Will*, a 1930s production, glorified the Nazis in general and Adolf Hitler in particular, and filmed versions of Shakespeare's nationalist plays helped stiffen British resolve after those same Nazis had overrun France in 1940 and seemed poised to invade England. Similarly, the U.S. government collaborated with Hollywood to produce patriotic stories for a country fighting World War II, most notably the *Why We Fight* series of films overseen by Frank Capra, one of the twentieth century's most popular and effective filmmakers. Films are not the only media used for this purpose. Television, radio and even public art, like statues and posters, and public events, like parades, are all mechanisms for the glorification of nations and leaders, which can help keep a society together. In short, a wide range of political systems do all they can to help educate (or, if you prefer, "indoctrinate") citizens about a country's greatness. Government officials use virtually any tool at hand to create and maintain this political support among those living within a nation's borders.

When Easton and Dennis (1969) considered how Americans develop this political support, they turned to American schoolchildren. A study using children to consider the development of political support made particular sense, given that the primary school years are very much a time when an individual begins to learn about his or her place in the world beyond the family: the world of classmates, communities and nations. Children are not all that likely to be directly subject to or to be aware of matters relating to specific support: There is no "quo" in the 'quid pro quo' of children who are far too young to vote. As expected, the feelings about government found among these children were indeed very general in nature.

> Initially children characteristically see the authorities as possible sources of nurturance, resources to which a person can turn in very much the same spirit that a child expects to be able to turn to his (or her) parents. (Easton and Dennis 1969:96)

> We find that the small child sees a vision of holiness when he (or she) chances to glance toward government—a sanctity and right-

ness of the demigoddess who dispenses the milk of human kindness. (Easton and Dennis 1969:137)

Under the Easton and Dennis approach, childhood emotional orientations toward government are thought to remain with people after they have become adults. These broad emotional attachments are part of what is called "diffuse support," one's general orientation to the overall political system. These early feelings are not irreversible, but they are powerful forces that are not swayed easily by subsequent events. This idea of the "primacy" of early learning went on to dominate studies of political socialization for decades (cf., Cook 1985).

At first it may seem strange to imagine that the values inculcated in childhood can have such a powerful influence throughout one's life. Even studies that found some change in values over time nevertheless showed a good deal of stability in attitudes and beliefs. This was true even during emotionally charged and rapidly changing political environments, like the 1960s (cf., Delli Carpini 1986; Jennings and Niemi 1968, 1974, 1981).

A good example of how powerful the lessons can be years later is seen in debates over whether it is constitutional to burn the American flag. Although the Supreme Court said such an act was a legal expression of one's First Amendment rights of free speech, many Americans reacted in horror to the Court's ruling, and candidates for public office have been proposing constitutional amendments to ban the practice for the dozen years since the Court's ruling in *Texas v. Johnson* (109 S. Ct. 2533 [1989]). The flag, as many former American elementary school students can recall, is a source of particular reverence in school classrooms. Many people can recall the exact words of the Pledge of Allegiance years, even decades, later, and a recent U.S. Court of Appeals for the Ninth Circuit ruling, which called for the words "under God" to be removed from the pledge, generated a huge public outcry (Lane 2002). Respect for the flag and the pledge persists in adulthood as a result of both the reverence for the flag shown in school and its presence at military, political and sporting events held throughout the country (and, if we include the Olympics, throughout the world). In the 1992 ANES, citizens were asked, "When you see the American flag flying how does it make you feel?" Only 3 percent said "not very good," while 44 percent said "extremely good," 35 percent said "very good" and 18 percent said "somewhat good." (This question was not asked in the 1996 ANES or the 2000 ANES).

While this project is a study of adult emotional and intellectual attachments to the U.S. political system, a discussion of the primacy of early learning is an important reminder of how profound some of the emotional attachments to politics may be in adults. This discussion also helps explain how resistant to change is public opinion regarding the political system in general, even as generations of individual politicians and government officials may disappoint and frustrate many citizens.

Not everyone who studies citizen discontent is enthusiastic about the Easton and Dennis approach, however. Stephen Craig (1993) has been one of the most effective critics of the diffuse/specific support dichotomy; he argued that if long-term attachments to government are affected by a pattern of poor governmental performance, how can one separate the two forms of citizen loyalty for analysis? While troubled by the diffuse/specific support model, Craig (1993:2) nevertheless considered the concept of political support a vital area for study, given the "pervasive negativism" that he said has replaced Americans' "traditional ambivalence" about politics in the United States in recent years. Other scholars who also are less than enthusiastic regarding the Easton and Dennis paradigm likewise have agreed that political support is an important area for scholars to research and try to understand (Stewart 1986; Parker 1986). Research using the political support questions developed by political scientists John R. Hibbing and Elizabeth Theiss-Morse (1995) demonstrate that these different political orientations can be considered separately (Farnsworth 1997, 2001b). Other researchers have also found much utility in the Easton and Dennis dichotomy (cf., Caldeira and Gibson 1992; Gibson and Caldeira 1992).

Despite these differences, political scientists from a variety of perspectives agree that citizen evaluations of the political system overall are more positive than might be expected given the high levels of citizen discontent expressed in public opinion regarding government officials and of citizen apathy registered in declining voting percentages. For all the public griping, expressed to pollster after pollster for the past thirty-some years, surveys of Americans' fundamental views of government show us to be a very loyal and a very patriotic people, as the discussion of flag burning and the controversy over the reciting of the Pledge of Allegiance above suggests.

POLITICAL SYSTEM SATISFACTION MEASURES

The 2000 version of the ANES provides us with the opportunity to consider public opinion concerning political support overall. The 1996 ANES offered two new questions that tap this vital sentiment—one asks whether the election was conducted fairly, the other asks broadly about how satisfied citizens are with current democratic practices in the United States. Both questions were asked also in the national survey conducted four years later. The ANES is the key resource used in this study.

The measures relating to general citizen satisfaction suggest public discontent is not centered on the overall political system. (Indeed, as we shall see in subsequent chapters, the focus of Americans' discontent is on the particular pieces of the political system rather than the polity as a whole.) When asked (the second question) about how they felt about the way democracy works in America, respondents in 2000 were overwhelmingly positive—only 15 percent said "not very satisfied" and only 4 percent said "not at all satisfied," leaving 81 percent of the survey respondents satisfied. This is a very high number given that this question was asked in the wake of the most contentious presidential election in a century. In 1996, a year without such a controversial presidential selection process, 81 percent of the citizens surveyed also said they were satisfied with the performance of democracy.

A bit greater frustration was seen in the other question, which asked whether the November 2000 election was conducted fairly. To this question 15 percent of the respondents said the 2000 presidential election was conducted very unfairly, and another 22 percent said it was conducted somewhat unfairly: reasonable responses given the highly political post-election strategies employed by both presidential candidates to try to emerge victorious (Ceaser and Busch 2001; Klain and Bash 2002; Tapper 2001, 2002; Terwilliger 2002). For more than a month, lawyers and election judges poured over ballots, as recounts were started, stopped and restarted until the Florida electoral mess finally was resolved in Bush's favor by the Supreme Court in a highly controversial 5–4 decision (cf., Bugliosi 2001).

With another 11 percent of the polled citizens considering the 2000 presidential election conducted in neither a clearly fair nor a clearly unfair way, a total of 52 percent considered the Gore-Bush deadlock to be conducted in a "very fair" or "somewhat fair" manner. In 1996, when Bill Clinton easily defeated Bob Dole, 49 percent said the election was "very fair" and another 26 percent said it was "somewhat fair." In other words, 75 percent of those surveyed in 1996 said the election was conducted in a fair way, nearly half again as many who reached that conclusion when assessing the much more problematic presidential election held four years later.

A third, somewhat different question asked citizens to evaluate the federal government on a 0–100 point scale, with 100 being the highest possible score. Less than one-third (28 percent) of those surveyed in 2000 gave the overall federal government a rating of below the midpoint of 50 on this "thermometer" scale, while 21 percent gave a reading of exactly 50, and 51 percent gave a score over 50 points. Few people gave either very high or very low responses: Only 8 percent of those surveyed gave the federal government a score of 25 or lower, while 16 percent gave a reading of 75 or above. A zero response was favored by 2 percent, while another 2 percent gave the government 100 points, the highest possible response. The response patterns in 2000 were similar to those of 1996, when 34 percent of those asked this question gave the government a score below the midpoint, 52 percent gave a score above midpoint and the remaining 14 percent gave the government a score of exactly 50.

As these questions indicate, there is a reservoir of goodwill among the public concerning the general operation of our society, a support that persists despite years of expressed frustration and even anger at governmental policies and political practices. This diffuse support, found even during periods of great anger like the weeks following the 2000 presidential election mess, is particularly important in terms of keeping the political system together in times of stress. Despite the expressed general frustration, despite the problematic nature of the 2000 election, a clear majority of Americans are disposed either positively or, at worst, neutrally in regard to the political system itself. (These questions were not asked in earlier versions of the ANES, and so one cannot compare public responses to these questions to years before 1996).

The generally positive evaluations of the overall political system are particularly impressive when one considers the depth of public objections to the performance of government officials. Table 2.1 illustrates the decline in political trust over the past forty years. These questions, which have been part of national surveys for decades, point to considerable contemporary public cynicism regarding the national government. While several measures of political trust (including some not shown in Table 2.1) show less mistrust in 2000 than in 1996, the overall pattern over the past several decades is still relatively negative. In 2000, 44 percent said the national government could be "trusted to do what is right" all or most of the time, a considerable rise from the 32 percent who expressed the same sentiment four years earlier. But both years demonstrate a far greater citizen cynicism than that seen in the 1960s and earlier. In 1964, in contrast, 78 percent said the government could be trusted. The most dramatic declines occurred during the years of Vietnam and Watergate, and public opinion generally stayed at those low levels in subsequent years. The last time at least half of the people surveyed thought the government could be trusted to do the right thing most of the time or nearly always was in 1972, the year of the Watergate break-in but well before the subsequent investigations and the White House cover-up drew more attention to the incident and led to a national crisis.

The other trust measure presented in Table 2.1 tells a similar story. In 2000, 65 percent of respondents thought the country was "run by a few big interests looking out for themselves," rather than for the benefit of all the people. This was a bit less negative than the 72 percent who thought the big interests ran things in 1996 and less negative than the 78 percent who thought the big interests dominated politics in 1992. But all three numbers represent a sharp decline from the 31 percent who thought the government worked primarily for the big interests in 1964.

Table 2.1
Patterns of Political System Trust, 1964–2000 (Presidential election years only)

Question: How much of the time do you think you can trust the government in Washington to do what is right—just about always, most of the time, or only some of the time?

	2000	1996	1992	1988	1984
JUST ABOUT ALWAYS	4%	2%	3%	4%	4%
MOST OF THE TIME	40%	30%	26%	37%	41%
SOME OF THE TIME	55%	67%	69%	56%	54%
NEVER (VOLUNTEERED)	1%	1%	2%	3%	1%

	1980	1976	1972	1968	1964
JUST ABOUT ALWAYS	2%	3%	5%	8%	15%
MOST OF THE TIME	24%	31%	49%	55%	63%
SOME OF THE TIME	70%	65%	45%	37%	22%
NEVER (VOLUNTEERED)	4%	1%	1%	0.2%	0.1%

Note: Percentages may not add up to 100% because of rounding.

In only one presidential year over the past quarter century—in 1984—did at least 40 percent of those surveyed believe that government worked primarily for the benefit of all.

In good times and bad, Americans are a cynical people. This is true when they consider whether they trust the government; this is also true when they consider whether citizens think the government pays attention to them. The questions of whether the government is thought to listen to ordinary citizens and whether ordinary citizens think they can influence the political process measure political efficacy, one of the most important citizen evaluations of government. People who think the gov-

Table 2.1(continued)

Question: Would you say the government is pretty much run by a few big interests looking out for themselves or that it is run for the benefit of all the people?

	2000	1996	1992	1988	1984
BIG INTERESTS	65%	72%	78%	67%	59%
BENEFIT OF ALL	35%	28%	21%	33%	41%

	1980	1976	1972	1968	1964
BIG INTERESTS	77%	73%	59%	44%	31%
BENEFIT OF ALL	23%	27%	41%	56%	69%

Note: Percentages may not add up to 100% because of rounding.

ernment listens to citizens and people who believe they could influence the political process if they tried to do so are said to have high levels of political efficacy. With political efficacy, as with political trust, we see that Americans have become disposed much more negatively toward government in recent years, as the results in Table 2.2 demonstrate.

In the 2000 ANES, citizens were not all that optimistic about the possibility that the national government was interested in what citizens wanted. In 2000, 40 percent gave a negative response, agreeing with the statement that "People like me don't have any say about what the government does." A total of 53 percent in the 2000 survey either disagreed somewhat or disagreed strongly, and another 8 percent neither agreed nor disagreed with the statement. Response patterns in recent years have been far more critical than the 30 percent who thought the government was not listening to citizens in 1964.

A similar pattern emerges for the other political efficacy question found in Table 2.2. People were asked in the 2000 ANES whether they agreed with the statement, "Public officials don't care much about what people like me think." In that most recent survey, 34 percent disagreed and thought government officials cared at least somewhat. As recently as 1984, 57 percent thought that government officials cared about what ordinary citizens thought. And in 1964, 63 percent disagreed with the negative statement and believed that public officials cared about the thoughts of ordinary citizens.

Table 2.2
Patterns of Political Efficacy, 1964–2000 (Presidential election years only)

Question: <Respondent [R] agrees/disagrees that . . . > People like me don't have any say about what the government does. (Fewer options were offered in 1984 and in earlier years.)

	2000	1996	1992	1988
AGREE STRONGLY	15%	14%	12%	15%
AGREE SOMEWHAT	25%	31%	24%	26%
NEITHER AGREE NOR DISAGREE	8%	10%	6%	9%
DISAGREE SOMEWHAT	39%	34%	33%	29%
DISAGREE STRONGLY	14%	12%	25%	21%

	1984	1980	1976	1972	1968	1964
AGREE	32%	40%	41%	41%	41%	30%
DISAGREE	68%	60%	59%	60%	59%	70%

Note: Percentages may not add up to 100% because of rounding.

The numbers found in Table 2.1 and Table 2.2 show a very similar pattern: Citizens are disposed far less positively toward government officials than they were in the mid-1960s and earlier. When it comes to issues of whether politicians can be trusted to do the right thing and whether they are listening to citizens, public opinion regarding elected officials has become far more negative over the final third of the twentieth century. Given these negative opinions regarding governmental performance, it may be surprising that citizens are disposed as positively as they are when evaluating the national government on a 0–100 point scale. But this distinction comes from the fact that citizens are being asked about two different things: How one feels about governmental performance is not the same thing as how one evaluates the overall political system in this country. Often, this difference is not considered sufficiently in the study of American public opinion.

Table 2.2 (continued)

Question: <Respondent [R] agrees/disagrees that . . . > (1964-1992) I don't think public officials care much what people like me think. (1996, 2000) Public officials don't care much about what people like me think. (Fewer options were offered in 1984 and in earlier years.)

	2000	1996	1992	1988
AGREE STRONGLY	19%	17%	16%	17%
AGREE SOMEWHAT	37%	44%	36%	34%
NEITHER AGREE NOR DISAGREE	11%	15%	10%	11%
DISAGREE SOMEWHAT	28%	21%	28%	30%
DISAGREE STRONGLY	6%	3%	10%	8%

	1984	1980	1976	1972	1968	1964
AGREE	43%	55%	54%	50%	44%	37%
DISAGREE	57%	46%	47%	50%	56%	63%

Note: Percentages may not add up to 100% because of rounding.

GENERATIONAL DIFFERENCES IN ORIENTATIONS TOWARD GOVERNMENT

Every political system eventually will come to depend on its younger citizens. This is particularly important to note in a long-standing democratic society such as the United States, where the nation's political cultures and values have been handed down through the centuries from one generation to the next. Failure on the part of a country to generate among younger citizens supportive feelings toward government could weaken a political system by eroding its perceived legitimacy. "Generation gaps" in political support can create pressure for a society in the short term and in the long term, as those younger generations grow into increased political prominence and older generations fade from the scene.

Generational differences in feelings about the government occur because people who are young at different times experience very different things. Generational differences occur as people from different age groups receive and react to external experiences in different ways. People who are voting for the first time, starting full-time work and otherwise securing independence from their families are likely to be particularly concerned with and influenced by current events and current conditions. Those citizens who have been evaluating varying conditions and different candidates for decades, on the other hand, may be affected less dramatically by current events and other short-term factors (Beck 1974; Delli Carpini 1986; Alwin, Cohen and Newcomb 1991).

Researchers have found many generation gaps throughout our nation's history, but the differences among today's adults have triggered the greatest interest (cf., Beck 1974; Delli Carpini 1986; Elazar 1976; Jennings and Niemi 1981; Strauss and Howe 1991). People who at an impressionable age saw their society undergo a dramatic event or a substantial transformation (including such things as the Great Depression, World War II, the Vietnam War and Watergate) have distinct experiences that distinguish them from older and younger groups, and members of each age-group are bound more closely to one another (Mannheim 1952; Delli Carpini 1986; Craig and Bennett 1997; cf., Jennings and Niemi 1981).

The differences in generational experiences can be stark. People who were born in the years after World War II entered adulthood during a time of heightened unrest in America—civil rights, Vietnam and then Watergate. They are likely to have a very different perspective on government than that of their parents, who might have credited the national government with ending the Depression and with winning World War II.

Children growing up in the United States are subject to considerable political socialization in the nation's classrooms—such things as the pictures of national heroes like George Washington and Abraham Lincoln on the walls and the reverence shown for the flag and the pledge are obvious examples. They are also subject to reenforcement of those ideas from parents and from peers often subject to the same influences. But, even in a democratic society, public and private pressures encouraging one to hold certain views and behave in certain ways do not disappear with age. Many researchers think that a second period of one's life— young adulthood—represents another time when one is quite susceptible to political influences. The years of young adulthood are sometimes referred to as "impressionable years" by political socialization scholars (Alwin, Cohen and Newcomb 1991). This theory suggests that when people leave the shelter of their childhood homes to live on their own, go to college or start their careers, the personal and political events of those first years of relative independence can have a dramatic influence on the people they become and the people they are likely to remain for the rest of their lives.

This theory also suggests considerable similarities within generations and considerable differences across generations in citizen orientations. Each generation, after all, has somewhat different formative experiences. As Duane F. Alwin, Ronald L. Cohen and Theodore Newcomb (1991) noted, the Bennington College students of the 1930s, women who came of age politically during the New Deal in the aggressively community oriented and highly progressive environment of Bennington, Vermont, were dramatically more liberal than women who entered their late teens and early twenties during the more economically and politically stable 1920s as well as those who followed the 1930s cohort. Further, the young women in the Bennington study were socialized directly to the liberal values that permeated the explicitly alternative, if not radical, Bennington curriculum and living environment. The Bennington women were mostly from wealthy families surviving the Depression in more or less good shape, and had they stayed at home, most likely they would have remained more conservative. Bennington taught them to be socially responsible and instilled liberal values in these students through the college's commitment to learning through experience and community activity. (Alwin, Cohen and Newcomb 1991).

The Depression and Bennington worked to shape the political orientations of these women in ways that were considerably at odds with their backgrounds, strong evidence for both the impressionable-years hypothesis and for the existence of a distinct generation shaped by the Depression (cf., Beck 1974). Most women in the Bennington College study, in fact, remained more liberal throughout their lives, even though many of them came from and returned to a world of considerable economic privilege where liberalism in general—and the New Deal in particular—was not received with much enthusiasm (Alwin, Cohen and Newcomb 1991).

Although this study focuses on the impressionable-years perspective of political socialization, two other competing perspectives on political learning merit some discussion. One approach, the life-cycle thesis, posits that aging is more important than age for explaining political attitudes and behavior. Life-cycle theories are sometimes based on the "primacy principle," which suggests that whatever is learned first—by children at home with their families, perhaps, or in elementary schools—is learned best (Hess and Torney 1967). While parts of how an individual relates to the political world, including emotional orientations toward the president that develop during childhood, the evidence regarding political socialization suggests that there can be significant political learning during the impressionable years of early adulthood as well (cf., Easton and Dennis 1969; Jennings and Niemi 1981; Alwin, Cohen and Newcomb

1991). This is consistent with the fact that some evaluations of government, particularly things like political trust and political efficacy, require a level of political sophistication that may escape children and adolescents too young to vote.

Both the impressionable-years thesis of generational differences and the primacy principle of life-cycle effects suggest that individual feelings become relatively stable once they have been formed. The other competing political socialization theory suggests that a person's orientations toward the political world are fixed neither in childhood nor in early adulthood, but instead remain open to new learning across one's lifetime (Kinder and Sears 1985). All people aware of a particular development occurring at a particular point in time may react in a similar fashion, regardless of their age or past experiences, according to this competing theory. This perspective does not appear all that relevant to the study of political support in recent years, however, given the generational differences in political orientations discussed in the coming pages.

Much of the work built on generational differences regarding political orientations in the United States involves the study of people who were young adults in the 1960s and are now 50 years old or more and on a distinct post–Baby Boom generation, whose oldest members are approaching their mid-40s. The Baby Boom generation, the largest ever produced in this country, is a natural generational group to consider, given its size and its distinct experiences during a young adulthood marked by disputes over civil rights, Vietnam and Watergate (cf., Jennings and Niemi 1974, 1981; Delli Carpini 1986). Indeed, it is exactly these defining issues that one would expect to play a particularly strong role in framing the views of members of this generation toward politics. People who came of age politically during the 1960s and 1970s would likely have very negative views about political figures in general, given the huge debates over the character and performance of Presidents Richard Nixon and Lyndon Johnson. But the fact that the institutions of American government eventually did work—state-sponsored segregation ended, U.S. troops were pulled out of Vietnam and Nixon was forced from office—may make them somewhat more supportive of the political system on an institutional level than otherwise might be expected.

This study will use the generational dividing lines drawn by William Strauss and Neil Howe (1991): the G.I. generation (born 1901–1924), the Silent generation (born 1925–1942), the Baby Boom cohort (born 1943–1960), and the group we will call the Next generation (born 1961–1981). These divisions, which are used regularly in political science, have the advantage over some of the other groupings used to define generations of being somewhat similar in size (cf., Beck 1984; Bennett and Bennett 1990; Bennett and Rademacher 1997; Craig and Bennett 1997).

This model creates a group of young adults, a Baby Boom generation and two pre–Boom generations. Popular accounts of today's young adults have tended to portray the Next generation (sometimes identified as Generation X) as especially alienated from mainstream politics (cf., Strauss and Howe 1991; Howe and Strauss 1993). More scholarly investigations have provided a more balanced perspective (cf., Dennis and Owen 1997; Owen and Dennis 1994; Craig and Bennett 1997). In the main, these evaluations have revealed generational differences mainly with respect to values, with many members of this youngest American voting group characterized as "ambivalent" (Owen and Dennis 1994).

The apparent lack of a galvanizing external political experience for this youngest generation suggests we should find a somewhat inconsistent pattern in their views about politics and considerable fluidity in those views over relatively short periods of time. Since recent years have been marked by the rise of the relatively cynical Baby Boomers to power in America, one might expect echoes of their negativity regarding government to lead to a steadily more negative orientation over time on the part of members of the Next generation.

Some might argue that the optimism of the Reagan years should have made these young adults quite idealistic. But in practice the influences felt during those years might have been more mixed. After all, for many young people the 1980s were not "morning in America." Many people who first entered the workforce in the 1980s suffered from underemployment, stagnant wage rates, a lack of job security and an expectation of material comfort that often exceeded what their salaries could provide (Howe and Strauss 1993; Rushefsky 1996). Of course, the Iran-Contra affair and exploding budget deficits also took some of the shine off the Reagan years. Given these conditions, one might expect members of the Next generation to think more like the cynical Boomers than the more optimistic older generations.

The two oldest generations in this study, including citizens who were born before the end of World War II, passed through their impressionable years during the years of some of America's greatest successes: the defeat of the depression and of Hitler and the massive postwar economic boom. They therefore would be likely to be disposed very positively about the country, particularly when it comes to overall evaluations of the political system.

This study will use ANES responses, when available, to questions asked in 1956, 1972 and 1988—the presidential election years in which a sufficiently large subsample (300 or more) of young voters from each of the Silent, Boom and Next generations became a part of the electorate. Those three selected years are equidistant, as they are sixteen years apart. (For some questions not asked in 1956, the 1958 responses are provided.) ANES responses in 1992, 1996 and 2000 also are presented to enhance our focus on recent trends in public opinion regarding the national government. The smallest overall sample for any year used here is 1,341 in 1956; the largest is 2,485 in 1992. The generational groups used in this study range in size from 945, the number of G.I. generation respondents in 1956, to 123, the number of G.I. generation respondents in 2000. (Because the G.I. generation group has become quite small with the passage of time, it is dropped from some parts of the analyses that follow.) The public opinion changes point to the younger generations' governmental views' importance to the country's future trajectory: Nearly three-quarters of the sample in 2000 are from the two youngest generational groups, the Baby Boomers and the post-Boom generation.

Given age differences, responses for all groups are not available for all years in the ANES. In 1956, after all, no one in the post-Boom generation had been born, and even the oldest Boomers were in their early teenage years.

Generational Differences in Evaluations of the Political System

Are younger generations more or less negative in their evaluations of the political system overall? Table 2.3 provides some insight on that question in 2000. In the top half of this table, evaluations of the national government on the 0–100 point thermometer scale are sorted by generational group. To make the results more comprehensible (who wants to look at a table with 101 rows?), the thermometer scores are condensed into five groups: very negative (0–20), somewhat negative (21–40), neutral (41–60), somewhat positive (61–80) and very positive (81–100). The results are clear: The two younger generations are considerably more negative than the two older generations. The Next generation has a smaller percentage of its respondents giving the federal government a rating of above 60 points than any of the other three generational groups, meaning that today's young adults are least likely to give the national government a passing grade. In fact, only one out of twenty members of this youngest generational group would give the government a score above 80, and fewer than one out of ten Baby Boomers would assess the government that highly. The most positive group, the G.I. generation, has three times the percentage of people giving a high score to the federal government than did the Next generation.

As would be expected for members of the group that is the least positive, they set the standard for the most negative generation. Thirty percent of the Next generation gave the government a score of 40 or below, more than double the percentage that the G.I. generation gave it. But the Next generation was not alone, as the Baby Boomers tied for the most negative generation on this measure. In the 2000 survey, the Baby Boomers are as likely as the Next generation to give the national government

Table 2.3
Generations and Federal Government Satisfaction

The federal government thermometer rating (0–100 scale) is condensed into five categories.

2000	NEXT	BOOM	SILENT	GI	CHI-SQUARE (signif)
81-100 HIGH	5%	9%	11%	16%	
61-80	22%	20%	27%	28%	
41-60 NEUTRAL	43%	41%	43%	42%	.00
21-40	22%	22%	16%	12%	
0-20 LOW	8%	8%	4%	2%	

Perceived Performance of Democracy (4 is the most positive response; 1 the least).

2000	NEXT	BOOM	SILENT	GI	CHI-SQUARE (signif)
4 HIGH	29%	29%	41%	45%	
3	51%	49%	45%	41%	.00
2	16%	18%	12%	10%	
1 LOW	5%	4%	3%	3%	

Note: Percentages may not add up to 100% because of rounding.

a rating of 40 or below, which can be interpreted as a somewhat negative or very negative assessment.

Why might the two oldest generations be the most positive about the federal government? They would be the citizen groups most familiar with the government's performance in the two major American crises of the twentieth century—the depression and World War II. These are issues likely to have touched people of those two generations deeply, particularly those who lived through those times during the highly impressionable ages of adolescence and early adulthood. One would expect older citizens to be the most positive if their perspectives were formed by such experiences. But the positive feelings may also be of a more recent vintage. Given the considerable number of retirees found in those two generations, one also may wonder whether national government programs like Social Security and Medicare may be part of the reason for the increased senior satisfaction. Unfortunately, the question was not asked before the 1996 ANES to allow for longer term analysis. (In the 1996 survey the generational patterns were quite similar to those seen for 2000, with the oldest groups most positive and the younger generations most negative.)

The second half of Table 2.3 provides a comparison for generational group evaluations on the question of democratic satisfaction. In the 2000 ANES, the largest percentage of the most dissatisfied are found in the two younger generations. More than one out of every five young adults (21 percent) in the Next generation said they were "not very satisfied or not at all satisfied with the way democracy works in the United States." The Boomers scored slightly more negatively, with 22 percent expressing less than satisfaction on this measure. For the older generations, 13 percent and 15 percent are found in these two most negative categories.

Despite the relatively large number of negative responses among the youngest adults, Table 2.3 also demonstrates that, overall, none of these generations are all that alienated. Four out of five members of the Next generation said they were satisfied or fairly satisfied with the way democracy works in this country. Likewise, a total of 78 percent of the Boomers were found in the two most positive groups. As one would expect, the results are even higher for other generations: eighty-six percent of those from each of the two oldest generations are found in the two most positive categories.

Both political support measures show a clear difference in generational group responses. The chi-square statistic, used by social scientists to test for statistically significant differences in survey responses, demonstrates that the differences among the responses of generational groups are substantial (a significance value of .05 or below qualifies as a statistically significant finding). The values here demonstrate that there are very large generational differences found in the responses to these questions.

But why might the younger groups be consistently the most negative? The 2000 results of these two measures may be the result of youthful optimism regarding the future, a belief that things can change (a thought that has occurred to a few other youthful generations over the years). Perhaps as members of the Next generation age they will be more satisfied with the current state of our democratic system. After all, one may be more anxious about the future at 20 or 30 years of age than at 50 or 60, when the passage of time may have reduced some of the uncertainties of life and perhaps some of one's youthful idealism (cf., Jennings and Niemi 1981; Delli Carpini 1986). One also may be more willing to accept the imperfections of a political system as one obtains more experience with it. Or perhaps not. After all, the Boomers—the generation that came of age during the contentious politics of the 1960s—provide evidence that anger generated in one's youth may not dissipate with time. The most satisfied generations, as measured here, were the oldest ones. This is consistent with the fact that that the two older generations passed through their impressionable years during times of much broader public support for government.

In our search for longer term trends, we cannot do much with these newer survey questions. Neither question has been asked frequently enough to perceive any long-term changes in responses among the different generational groups. In order to make such comparisons, we will return to the measures of political trust and efficacy introduced earlier in the chapter. These questions have been asked for decades, and so we will be able to see generational differences in recent years. We will also be able to see how today's older citizens answered these questions when they were young adults and compare their responses to those of today's young adults.

Returning to political system trust, for example, we find in Table 2.4 that the cynicism of this youngest generation had increased since 1988, the first year when a substantial number of post-Boomers were old enough to vote and to be included in surveys like the ANES. The percentage of people in the Next Generation who said they could trust the government only some or none of the time increased from 57 percent in 1988 to 72 percent in 1992 before falling back to 69 percent four years later. The figure fell to 62 percent in 2000 for this group. Although the numbers for this youngest group were less negative in the 2000 ANES than in some earlier years, the most recent figures represent a clear majority of negatively disposed citizens in the Next generation. Indeed, it was the most negative generation on this question. In addition, other generations saw much greater declines in negativity between 1992 and 2000.

The evidence here suggests that younger citizens have caught up with and even passed the cynicism of their elders. Indeed, the chi-square statistic used to check for generational differences on that item finds that in the 2000 ANES these generational differences were statistically signif-

Table 2.4
Generations and Political System Trust

Question: How much of the time do you think you can trust the government in Washington to do what is right—just about always, most of the time, or only some of the time? (Percentages listed relate to those who said "only some" or volunteered "none of the time")

	NEXT	BOOM	SILENT	GI	CHI-SQUARE (signif)
2000	62%	59%	46%	47%	.00
1996	69%	70%	66%	61%	n.s.
1992	72%	70%	70%	70%	n.s.
1988	57%	61%	53%	64%	.02
1972	--	43%	43%	49%	.02
1958	--	--	24%	22%	n.s.

Note: Not all percentages could be calculated for all generation groups in all years.

icant (though the generational differences were not significant in either 1996 or 1992).

Because these questions have been asked for many years, we can compare today's young generations with the young generations of the past. Younger citizens in 1972 (the Baby Boom generation) tended to be more optimistic when they first entered the electorate, but they became more cynical as the years passed. The change was more pronounced for the Boomers, but the same basic trend can be found for the members of the Next generation. When the Silent generation first entered the electorate (shown in this table by the 1958 survey results), it offered the national government far more political trust than either of these two younger generations at comparable points in the life cycle (1972 for the Boomers and 1988 for the Next generation).

The rapid increase in youth cynicism measured here suggests the utility of the impressionable-years approach. Younger citizens have greater fluidity in their opinions and show greater changes between 1988 and 2000, perhaps because they have had little time to form more permanent opinions regarding the political world.

The ANES political efficacy questions, like this study's measures of political trust, allow for extensive across-time comparisons. The results are found in Table 2.5.

Table 2.5
Generations and Political Efficacy

Question: <R agrees/disagrees that . . . > Public officials don't care much about what people like me think. (Percentages listed are of those who agreed and who strongly agreed)

	NEXT	BOOM	SILENT	GI	CHI-SQUARE (signif)
2000	56%	53%	59%	57%	n.s.
1996	56%	58%	66%	71%	.00
1992	51%	49%	56%	59%	.00
1988	48%	49%	49%	60%	.00
1972	--	45%	46%	55%	.00
1956	--	--	22%	26%	n.s.

Note: Not all percentages could be calculated for all generation groups in all years.

In one way, the findings here for the youngest generation could not be more different. Since agreement with these statements is a negative evaluation of governmental performance, the lowest percent of agreement represents the most positive generation. For the question known as "no care," the Next generation was in the middle of the pack. (The generational differences on this measure in 2000 are not statistically significant.) For this efficacy question we do find an increased cynicism on the part of this youngest age cohort. In the cases of this measure, however, all age groups have become less optimistic over the past four presidential elections. The starting levels in 1988 for the Next generation are similar to the starting levels in 1972 for the Baby Boom generation, and both were far more negative regarding governmental responsiveness than either of the other generation groups who responded to this question in 1956, when even the oldest Baby Boomers were in middle school and many of them had not yet been born. When today's seniors answered questions in the 1956 surveys, the oldest members of the Next generation would not be born for another five years (cf., Farnsworth 2003b).

Where Do the Overall Evaluations of Government Come From?

The results here generally have shown that people of different generations come to very different conclusions regarding the political system. When asked to evaluate the national government on a 0–100 point scale and when asked to express how well they thought democracy worked in this country, the two youngest generational groups were the least positive, while the two older groups were the most positive (see Table 2.3). This pattern, found for both of those overall political support measures, is consistent with the impressionable-years hypothesis. Older citizens, weaned on the government's successes in battling the depression and the Nazis, continue to find themselves far more positive in their evaluations of the political system than those citizens who entered adulthood during the more negative times marked by such things as Vietnam and Watergate and their aftermaths. While it would be an exaggeration to say that the younger generations are overwhelmingly negative on either measure, passage of time will remove some of today's most positively disposed citizens from the electorate (as they are the most advanced in age). Will the Next generation become more positive as it becomes a more influential voice in the American polity? Who knows? But if one looks at the patterns of more specific political evaluations of government, including such things as political trust and political efficacy, the evidence suggests that generations become more cynical, not less, as they leave their early adulthood behind.

But one important question remains in this examination of citizen orientations toward the overall political system: From where do these federal government thermometer and democratic satisfaction evaluations come? The simple answer is that they come from the mouths of people surveyed by interviewers from the ANES. But we are after a more sophisticated response than that. The overall values expressed in responses to these two questions likely spring from other political orientations, perhaps from factors in a person's background: gender, race and partisan identification with Democrats, Republicans or Independents. Perhaps the other measures discussed here—citizen opinions regarding political efficacy and political trust—can predict also one's overall level of democratic satisfaction.

In chapter 1, three major perspectives relating to citizen discontent were presented. The first was demand overload, the idea that citizens have overburdened modern Western democracies with too many demands, and demands that are too complex to be resolved easily. The second was procedural frustration, the idea that citizens are very frustrated with the cumbersome and distant procedures of lawmaking. The third focused on the declining civic community (the "bowling alone" thesis) and suggested that citizens are getting increasingly frustrated with government because society itself is breaking down and more and more people separate from their fellow citizens and their neighbors.

The final two tables of this chapter allow us to compare the effectiveness of the three approaches. The tables include overall results as well as separate results for the three youngest generational groups. If you expect the demand overload model will be an effective explanation, look for the effectiveness of survey questions that relate to governmental competence, which is measured in these tables by citizen evaluations of economic performance and foreign policy. Drawing on the impressionable-years idea, one would expect that political competence would be important for all generations, though the youngest generation would likely be most concerned with economic matters. The Next generation's economic condition, after all, may be the most vulnerable to economic downturns as its members have not had the time to advance as far in a job or to save as much money as their elders have had. Given the experiences of their young adulthood, the older generations—such as the Silent generation, many members of which reached adulthood during the height of the Cold War (from the late 1940s until the Cuban Missile Crisis of 1962)—seem likely to be focused on foreign policy concerns, as would many of the Baby Boomers, who faced Vietnam during their "impressionable years."

People who expect the second theory, the procedural frustration explanation, to be an effective model would favor the political trust questions. Political trust should be an important measure for establishing political support in general and for the two youngest generations in particular. The generations that entered adulthood during and after the years of Vietnam and Watergate were exposed to much more public cynicism about government than people who became adults in more optimistic times.

Supporters of the third theory, that of the the declining civic community, should focus on measures of interpersonal trust, which measures how favorably a respondent views his or her fellow citizens. One may hypothesize that interpersonal trust would be particularly salient to political support among the youngest citizens. Such a pattern would be consistent with the observations that younger adults often focus on more localized and community-oriented concerns, as in the "Think Globally, Act Locally" perspective that has arisen in recent years (cf., Howe and Strauss 1993; Strauss and Howe 1991).

Table 2.6 provides the overall ordinary least squares (OLS) regression results for the federal government thermometer rating as the political support dependent variable as well as columns for three of the four generational groups discussed above (there were too few members of the oldest [G.I.] generation in the 2000 survey to allow for effective OLS regression analysis). The thermometer rating is the dependent variable because we predict that the value a person chooses between zero and 100 depends on a number of factors: race, gender, education, perceived

Table 2.6
Support for the Federal Government and Generations: OLS Regression Analysis

2000	Unstandardized Coefficients (b)			
	ALL	NEXT	BOOM	SILENT
Education	-.51	.37	-.85	-.19
Income	-.29	-.63*	.12	-.53
Sex	1.99	.53	2.89	1.26
White	-2.88	-3.03	-1.92	-8.10
African American	8.24***	6.96	13.18**	-3.69
Folded Party ID	1.47**	2.71**	-.12	1.94
Folded Ideology	-.45	-.99	-.06	.01
Political Trust Index	2.93***	2.40***	3.69***	2.64***
Efficacy Index	-.12	.18	-.52	-.11
Economy Past Year	1.05*	1.28	.21	.06
Economy Next Year	.42	-.37	1.32	1.30
U.S. World Position	1.20**	1.06	1.59**	1.49
Responsiveness Index	3.20***	1.84*	4.27***	2.74*
Interpersonal Trust Index	.04	.12	-.18	-.20
Adjusted R-sq.	.22***	.16***	.28***	.15***
n	1086	410	402	204

* $p < .05$ ** $p < .01$ *** $p < .001$

governmental competence, political trust and a person's perspective on human nature. Information for the questions used here can be found in Appendix A.

This table is more difficult to read than the others in this chapter—in fact, the OLS regression models presented here are the most complicated statistical technique presented in this book—so a bit of explanation on how to read this table may be helpful. To begin, look to the bottom of the table for the adjusted r-square. This overall model performance statistic measures how well the independent variables in the equation, when taken together, can predict the value of the dependent variable. We can compare the various r-squares here to see that the independent variables are most effective at predicting the dependent variable values of Baby Boomers (adjusted r-square = .28) and worst at predicting the values of the Silent generation (adjusted r-square = .15). Since you don't have to understand the mechanics of this technique to interpret the results, suffice it to say that all of these models are statistically significant, and all have relatively good predictive power when compared to other research involving public opinion.

But which variables matter in these equations? Here, the asterisks are the key. Any number followed by an asterisk means that the related independent variable is statistically significant, that is, it helps predict the value a person gives the federal government on that thermometer scale. Consider the "all" column, the far left column of coefficients in Table 2.6. Two background measures—one's intensity of partisan feelings and whether a respondent was African American—were statistically significant predictors of the values offered for the dependent variable, the "thermometer" evaluation of the federal government. Strong Republicans and strong Democrats, that is, those with high partisan intensity, had higher evaluations of the national government, as did African Americans.

A number of other measures were also important: the political trust index, the perceived economic performance over the past year, the response to the U.S. position in the world and the perceived governmental responsiveness index. (An index adds the results of several related questions into a single combined measure, which is more effective and less cumbersome than a group of single measures. For example, the two political trust questions discussed above—Does the government do the right thing? and Does it look out for ordinary citizens?—are combined with other related measures to create a political trust index. A listing of the ANES questions combined into indices is found in Appendix A.)

The overall results here support both the demand overload and procedural frustration perspectives, though not the declining civic community model. The interpersonal trust measures fail to be of statistical significance in the overall model, and they also are not significant for any of these tests involving the generational subgroups.

The generational groups sometimes focus on different issues when considering political support. While all three groups focus on political trust, the Boomers are the only generation for whom America's standing in the world is also highly significant, perhaps because of the international crises that took place during the formative years of the Boomers—the days of the Cuban Missile Crisis and of the war in Vietnam. Perceived governmental responsiveness matters for all three groups, but is most powerfully relevant to the assessments of the Baby Boomer generation, a generation particularly inclined in its youth toward trying to make itself heard in the political world (Delli Carpini 1986; Jennings and Niemi 1974, 1981).

The importance of background measures, including race, intensity of party identification (party ID) and intensity of ideology, differs from generation to generation. African American Boomers are highly politicized, as one would expect, given that many African Americans of this generation came of age during the high-water mark of civil rights activism. It should come as no surprise that African Americans of this generation give the federal government high marks, as much of the advances in civil rights occurred because of federal government pressure against segregationist states and localities. For the youngest group, the most important background measures are partisan intensity and income, with the poorer partisans more positively disposed toward the federal government.

These findings give some indication of the difficulties government officials would face were they to try to improve the government's public standing. Citizens can be demanding: To build political support, the government must be trustworthy, it must be responsive, it must do a good job on the economy and it must keep America strong in the world. The findings here are consistent with research that suggests that the declining role played by political parties in the polity undermines effective citizen links to government (cf., Patterson 1993).

Table 2.7 uses the perceived fairness of the 2000 election as the dependent variable representing political support. It uses the same independent variables used to predict the values given by individual citizens on the government evaluation thermometer, except it uses unfolded measures of partisanship and ideology. The unfolded measures were used here because how one felt about the highly controversial postelection selection in the 2000 presidential contest was likely to depend considerably on one's partisan loyalties. Like Table 2.6, Table 2.7 provides both overall results (the "all" column) and separate models for the three youngest generational groups. The overall results here show support for both the procedural frustration and the declining civic community models. Higher levels of political trust, political efficacy and governmental responsiveness (procedural frustration) all lead to higher levels of political support, as does higher levels of interpersonal trust.

Once again, there are important generational differences. When its members evaluate the national government, the Boomer generation cares a great deal about political trust, political responsiveness and political efficacy, while the Next generation is concerned largely with political efficacy and interpersonal trust. Interpersonal trust is also important for the Silent generation, the oldest generation analyzed in Table 2.7. As expected, partisanship colors one's assessment of the 2000 presidential election: Republicans overall, as well as Republican members of the Next

Table 2.7
Perceived Fairness of Elections and Generations: OLS Regression Analysis

2000	Unstandardized Coefficients (b)			
	ALL	NEXT	BOOM	SILENT
Education	.08**	.04	.03	.20**
Income	.002	.02	-.001	-.04
Sex	-.25**	-.13	-.43**	-.19
White	-.05	-.08	.17	-.19
African American	-.44*	-.50	-.23	-.19
Party ID	.10***	.09*	.13**	04
Ideology	.04	.02	.05	.05
Political Trust Index	.08***	.07	.12**	.07
Efficacy Index	.07***	.08**	.07**	.06
Economy Past Year	-.04	-.03	-.03	-.01
Economy Next Year	-.01	-.04	.01	-.10
U.S. World Position	.03	-.07	.02	-.06
Responsiveness Index	.07	-.01	.14*	.03
Interpersonal Trust Index	.04***	.04**	.03*	.08***
Adjusted R-sq.	.19***	.15***	.21***	.26***
n	1014	399	369	184

* $p < .05$ ** $p < .01$ *** $p < .001$

generation and the Boomers, had more positive assessments of the fairness of the 2000 presidential contest than did Democrats.

Among the other background measures, in the overall model both women and African Americans were disposed more negatively regarding the conduct of the election, a result that could have been predicted, given the gender and racial gaps in presidential elections. In the overall model the higher educated citizens were more inclined to view the election as fair, though this pattern achieved statistical significance only in the Silent generation model.

Generally speaking, these results suggest the magnitude of the challenge government officials face in their efforts to improve political support. Simply put, this chapter demonstrates that the younger generations make more demands upon national government than does the older generation.

CONCLUSION

The political support questions contained in the 2000 ANES do not allow for an extensive over-time analysis; nor do they permit confident predictions concerning the future trajectory of political support. In particular, researchers cannot yet sort out the complications involved in determining whether the generational or life-cycle perspective is the more effective model for explaining generational differences (cf., Alwin, Cohen and Newcomb 1991; Hess and Torney 1967; Jennings and Niemi 1981). Perhaps as younger generations become older their political support will resemble more the orientations of today's seniors. Perhaps today's young adults will continue to be very demanding about governmental performance and its trustworthiness as they age. It is important, however, to note the current distinct orientations of these generational groups and to consider the importance of these citizen orientations toward the national government in the future.

A one-time snapshot of political support in 2000 can serve as the basis for some tentative conclusions about political support, both as it stood in that contentious year and as it may stand in the years ahead. The results here suggest that the national government, which is the least enthusiastically received by the younger generations, has a great deal of work to do when it comes to restoring political support. These younger generations expect high-quality government performance on a variety of measures: responsiveness, political trust, political efficacy and, above all, economic stewardship. Even interpersonal trust can affect their assessments of governmental performance.

The importance of economic matters, seen in Table 2.6, is consistent with the extensive research that has indicated that public feelings about government—and particularly incumbent officeholders—are tied closely to the health of the economy (cf., Lewis-Beck and Rice 1992). But the economic issue may have been less significant in the 2000 election than in other years, as fewer citizens appeared to consider it an important issue that year than in previous electoral contests (Campbell 2001; Wlezien 2001). Likewise, Gore did not emphasize the Clinton administration's economic performance in his presidential campaign, an approach that might have reduced the influence of this measure on voter perspectives in 2000 (Ceaser and Busch 2001; Farnsworth and Lichter 2003).

Overall, the results here demonstrate the utility of the impressionable-years model of generational socialization for explaining citizen opinion formation. Political support orientations could be predicted by considering the circumstances of the time citizens enter adulthood and the world of citizenship. Political trust mattered in a number of circumstances, but never more so than for the Boomers, who came of age during the times of Vietnam and Watergate. The less deferential younger generations likewise applied feelings of political efficacy to assessments of government.

The evidence from this 2000 survey offers some support for all three models: procedural frustration, demand overload and the declining civic community perspectives. The results demonstrate the magnitude of what citizens expect of government now and are likely to expect from government in the years ahead. While the task before the U.S. government seems daunting, many other countries face far more intense levels of citizen discontent. After all, most Americans in all generations are disposed favorably toward the U.S. political system, at least in its relatively abstract dimensions. Citizens have expressed a great deal of frustration with governmental performance in recent years, and the results here suggest that these frustrations are widespread and exist in different age-groups for different reasons. But there is no indication that any of these generational cohorts are totally disenchanted. In general, this is good news for people concerned about the legitimacy of our constitutional order.

Nevertheless, there may be serious trouble on the horizon. The youngest generation has been getting disposed more negatively toward the government over time, and the relative youthful idealism that was so much in evidence for some measures—including trust and efficacy—in the 1988 ANES had reduced by 2000. On some measures, the youngest citizens were among the most cynical. Members of the Baby Boom generation have taken over much of the national political scene from their elders, and they tend to be most like the youngest group in their negativity on some issues. The groups whose members were the most satisfied with the democratic system and with the federal government are exactly those whose generations are becoming progressively less influential and less numerous with the passage of time. The generations becoming more influential every year (the two younger groups) not only are the most negative, but also have the widest ranges of governmental demands relating to political support. The current state of political support is not all that good, particularly among younger citizens, and the findings from 2000 offer a caution for the future. If the public views seen in this chapter are replicated in studies of future years, or if political support trends downward through generational replacement, the consequences of government's failure to address these matters could be severe.

3

"Broken Branches?":
Support for the Component Parts
of Government

INTRODUCTION

The previous chapter not only demonstrated that there is considerable citizen frustration with government, but it also provided evidence that there are generally positive public feelings for the U.S. political system as a whole. There were some warning signs of potential problems in the future—most notably, the youngest generational groups often were found to be the most cynical about the political system—but the evidence so far shows that the American political system receives widespread acceptance, particularly in the abstract. Although the evidence offered in chapter 2 focused on public opinion in 2000, previous research along these same lines during the highly politically combative years of the mid-1990s showed very similar patterns (cf., Farnsworth 1997, 2000, 2001b, 2003b).

But citizens do not always look at their political system in the abstract, as a unified collective of political principles and institutions. There is ample evidence that citizens often do differentiate, particularly when one considers such things as widespread ticket splitting and the continuing popularity of divided government (cf., Fiorina 1992). Diffuse support, the public's general orientation toward the political system, is an important area to examine, but so too is specific support, the support directed at specific political authorities largely through their specific performance in office (Easton and Dennis 1969). What we are talking about here is the quid pro quo of politics; Presidents who are popular because they receive credit for a booming economy is one frequent example (cf., Lewis-Beck and Rice 1992).

Looking at both the political system itself and its component parts seems the only sound way to consider how attached Americans are to their political system and its leaders. To do otherwise hardly seems wise. Even the youngest children, after all, are able to distinguish among different political figures and institutions in past research of political support (Easton and Dennis 1969). That finding suggests that lumping the entire political system together for purposes of political support could not begin to offer the whole story (cf., Hibbing and Theiss-Morse 1995, 1998; Lowi 1985; Owen and Dennis 1990). To consider separately the various components of the political system seems necessary even for children, much less for adults (Easton and Dennis 1969).

This chapter examines separately the three branches of the national government: the executive, the legislative and the judicial. Most of the information provided here comes from surveys conducted during 2000, when Democrat Bill Clinton was completing his second term as president, when the Republican Party controlled both chambers of the U.S. Congress and when seven of the nine members of the U.S. Supreme Court were appointed by Republican presidents (though the court's members often align themselves—as they did in *Bush v. Gore*—into a 5–4 split favoring conservatives). Using the same basic approach developed in chapter 2, we will look at where political support for each of these branches originates. We also will use the same generational dividing lines employed in the previous chapter to examine generational differences involving that political support.

SUPPORT FOR THE PRESIDENCY

More than three decades ago, when political scientists asked youngsters about what the president does, even young children could identify the president as the national leader and as the public's protector (Easton and Dennis 1969). In the minds of children, "the president flies in on angel wings, smiling, beneficent, powerful, almost beyond the realm of mere mortals" (Easton and Dennis 1969:171). As children become older, their political understandings become more sophisticated, and they come to realize that there are limits on presidential power, including the limits enforced by members of Congress and the courts. But that powerful youthful socialization represented by the Pledge of Allegiance, by pictures of George Washington and Abraham Lincoln on the walls, may be quite influential, even into adulthood (Easton and Dennis 1969; Hess and Torney 1967; Jennings and Niemi 1974, 1981). In fact, these early lessons may help explain why even adults are more likely to approve of a president—any president—in times of war or other national crises (Gallup 2002; Lowi 1985; Nincic 1997). This is called the "rally 'round the flag effect," and this public opinion effect is so powerful that it has been found to occur even in cases of a high-visibility television movie, *The Day After*, a fictional story of nuclear war (Adams et al. 1994).

President George W. Bush's poll standings in late 2001 and early 2002 provide a recent example of this trend of greater public approval of a president during a national crisis. Bush's poll numbers, which had been in the mid-fifties throughout most of 2001, shot up dramatically in the wake of the September 11, 2001, terrorist attacks and remained above 80 percent for several months (Gallup 2002). Bush's numbers eventually began sinking as citizens increasingly turned their attention to the country's economic decline and paid less attention to the terrorist crisis, which seemed to have abated with the defeat of the Taliban in Afghanistan in the months after the hijackings (Stevenson and Elder 2002, Kohut 2002).

Theodore J. Lowi (1985) is one of many political scientists who believes that those childhood lessons of an admirable president remains with people throughout life and can affect citizen orientation to politics as adults. Many public feelings about government are tied to the president, who, in the minds of many citizens, has become a "lobbyist for all the people" and, in effect, the center of American government. Citizen expectations of government rely heavily on the president's performance, according to Lowi. Increasingly, presidents have been unable to satisfy public demands and have turned instead to public relations if not outright deceit to provide the appearance of White House political success. This, in turn, leads to a "pathology" in which each president overpromises and eventually faces exposure as a failure or a fraud or both (Lowi 1985). The pattern can be seen through Lyndon Johnson's efforts to minimize the economic consequences of the Vietnam War, through Richard Nixon's secret plan to end that war, through Jimmy Carter's promise that he would never lie as president and through the promises of both Ronald Reagan and George W. Bush that large tax cuts would not lead to massive federal budget deficits (Cook 2002; Lowi 1985; Neustadt 1990; Stevenson 2002; Weisman 2002; Woodward 1999).

Both matters of war and of the economy consistently have proven to be key factors in the level of presidential approval enjoyed—or not enjoyed—by recent occupants of 1600 Pennsylvania Avenue (Campbell 1992; Erikson, MacKuen and Stimson 2001; Lewis-Beck and Rice 1992). Ronald Reagan was elected president in 1980 in large measure because of public concerns that the American economy had declined during the four years of Jimmy Carter's presidency (Schneider 1981). Reagan, in fact, sought in 1980 to bring public anxiety regarding the economy to the surface, asking viewers in one debate, "Are you better off than you were four years ago?" (Hunt 1981). President George H.W. Bush enjoyed extremely high public approval ratings in the wake of the 1991 Persian Gulf War, but his reelection campaign—and his poll numbers—ran aground on a troubled economy (Ceaser and Busch 1993). Bob Dole, the Republican Party's 1996 nominee for president, was unable to derail Bill Clinton's reelection campaign, which was being fueled by steady economic growth (Ceaser and Busch 1997). In fact, Bill Clinton's ability to survive Republican attempts to drive him from office in the wake of the 1998 Clinton-Lewinsky scandal and the failed cover-up may have been due to the considerable public support the president retained during the scandal, thanks in part to his handling of the economy over the first five years of his presidency (Quirk and Cunion 2000; Owen 2000; Sabato, Stencel and Lichter 2000).

The focus of public expectations on the presidency is not entirely fair, as citizens tend to expect more than presidents reasonably can be expected to deliver. The American political system considerably limits presidential power by having separate political institutions share power (Fiorina 1992; Neustadt 1990; Jones 1994, 1995). But fair or not, the evidence is clear: Presidents are expected to deliver, particularly on the economy and on foreign policy/military matters, if they are to receive much public support.

Generational Differences in Presidential Approval

Table 3.1 provides a comparison of approval for President Clinton in 2000 for the four generational groups we have been using. Clinton is evaluated on the 0–100 point thermometer scale, condensed into five categories. Based on the political socialization trends previously identified, we would expect that older citizens, who came to adulthood in the less politically combative years before the mid-1960s, would be inclined most positively.

Members of the G.I. generation, who were born before 1925, did indeed view Clinton the most positively. A total of 28 percent of the people in this generational group gave Clinton a score of 81 or higher on the 0–100 point scale, slightly above the 25 percent of the members of the Silent generation (born 1925–1942) who rated Clinton that highly. The two younger generational groups, the Baby Boomers (born 1943–1960) and the Next generation (born 1961–1981), were notably less enthusiastic, with only 19 percent and 18 percent respectively giving Clinton a score of 81 or above. The significance of the chi-square statistic shows that the differences in Clinton approval ratings for the four generational groups are large enough to achieve statistical significance (the significance value should be .05 or less in political science research).

America's oldest citizens not only were brought up in a more patriotic time, but they also were brought up in a time of stronger political partisanship among the mass public (Campbell et al. 1980 [1960]; Dennis and Owen 1997; Miller 1992; Nie, Verba and Petrocik 1979). We see evidence here of that socialization effect as well. The oldest generational group, which had the greatest percentage of people in the most positive group, also had the greatest percentage of people in the most negative

Table 3.1
Generations and Approval of President Clinton

The Clinton approval thermometer rating (0-100 scale) is condensed into five categories.

2000	NEXT	BOOM	SILENT	GI	CHI-SQUARE (signif)
81-100 HIGH	18%	19%	25%	28%	
61-80	25%	24%	18%	18%	
41-60 NEUTRAL	23%	21%	20%	22%	.02
21-40	17%	15%	17%	8%	
0-20 LOW	17%	20%	21%	24%	

Note: Percentages may not add to 100% because of rounding.

group. As will be demonstrated shortly, partisanship can play a powerful role in the assessment of presidential and other political figures. Bill Clinton was an unusually polarizing figure, but the general pattern seen here has been seen elsewhere: Democrats tend to view a Democratic president more favorably than do Republicans, and vice versa. For more than four decades, most political scientists have viewed partisanship as a filter through which an individual's assessments of political figures is refined (cf., Campbell et al. 1980 [1960]). Younger generations, whose members came to adulthood during times of greater ticket splitting by voters, of increased prominence of political independents and of reduced general partisan attachments, were less likely to give Clinton a score of 20 or below. The G.I. generation seemed to have in relatively short supply people who had less extreme views of the former president. Only 48 percent of the members of the oldest generation gave Clinton a score between 21 and 80, as compared to 65 percent of the Next generation and 60 percent of the Baby Boomers.

These broad patterns of general differences presented above regarding President Clinton tell us part of what we need to know about presidents and political support. We now turn to an OLS regression analysis to determine more precisely the factors that relate to one's evaluation of Bill Clinton during his final months in office.

What Explains Public Approval of the President?

Given the above discussion, we can expect to see several general trends when we examine the factors that affect public evaluations of Bill Clinton. To begin, past research suggests we should see powerful links between how well the president is thought to have handled the economy and foreign/military policy and how positively he is viewed. Partisanship and ideology should also matter, with liberals and Democrats more likely to view Clinton positively than conservatives and Republicans.

Table 3.2 shows an OLS regression equation examining the factors relating to support for Bill Clinton for all survey respondents, with separate analyses conducted for the three youngest generational group (there were too few members of the G.I. generation in the 2000 ANES to analyze them further). This tables uses the same variables used in chapter 2, except that both partisanship and ideology are now unfolded to take account of the more partisan evaluations likely to occur when partisan figures are assessed.

Looking at the overall results, we see a very strong model: The adjusted r-square is .51. How one felt about Bill Clinton as president could be predicted very effectively by one's partisanship, ideology, race and level of political trust as well as by how well the president is perceived to have handled the economy and issues of foreign policy. As expected, people who thought the economy was improving and that the United States had grown stronger in the world rated the president highly, as did African Americans, liberals and Democrats. People who had high levels of political system trust also rated the president highly. Neither governmental responsiveness nor interpersonal trust seemed to have any relationship to public evaluations of Bill Clinton in 2000.

Turning now to generational differences, one can see that the questions used here work well for predicting the support of Clinton among all age groups. Four variables are significant for all three groups: party identification, ideology, the levels of political system trust and the country's position in the world. By comparing the size of the coefficients, one can observe that partisanship, ideology and political trust were important to members of the Silent generation, as one might have expected given the stronger partisan loyalties felt by older Americans. (The particular importance of partisanship and ideology to the assessment of Clinton by this older group also help explain why there were more very positive and more very negative evaluations among older Americans than among younger citizens.) The position of the United States in the world was more important in 2000 to evaluations of Clinton by members of the Boomers and the Silent generation than today's younger adults, perhaps

Table 3.2
Support for President Clinton and Generations: OLS Regression Analysis

2000	Unstandardized Coefficients (b)			
	ALL	NEXT	BOOM	SILENT
Education	-.28	-.71	.60	-.31
Income	-.18	.02	.08	-.45
Sex	-1.33	-3.85	.60	-1.24
White	-2.20	.15	-3.74	-3.43
African American	9.26**	13.01**	10.31*	3.36
Party ID (Unfolded)	-6.98***	-6.02***	-6.87***	-8.60***
Ideology (Unfolded)	-2.41***	-2.31***	-1.99**	-2.77**
Political Trust Index	1.68***	1.55**	1.69**	2.09*
Efficacy Index	-.14	.17	-.45	-.25
Economy Past Year	2.14***	3.59***	1.15	1.76
Economy Next Year	-.37	-.71	.48	-2.14
U.S. World Position	3.15***	3.13***	3.67***	3.53**
Responsiveness Index	-.14	.57	-.02	-2.55
Interpersonal Trust Index	.09	-.27	.33	.24
Adjusted R-sq.	.51***	.46***	.54***	.58***
n	1103	415	404	209

* $p < .05$ ** $p < .01$ *** $p < .001$

because the older generations came of age during the days of Soviet–U.S. animosity, and the proxy wars fought by communist and capitalist (or at least anti-communist) factions in Korea, Vietnam, Afghanistan, Nicaragua and elsewhere during the 1950s, 1960s, 1970s and early 1980s. Economic matters were significant to evaluation of Clinton only for the youngest group, the group with the largest number of newer employees (or for those in college, the soon-to-be employed). Such current and future young workers may be on a less-secure footing with their employers in what can sometimes be a last-hired, first-fired workplace culture. African Americans in the Baby Boom generation, the group most affected by the civil rights movement, and the Next generation, were more in-

clined to support Clinton than African Americans in the Silent generation.

A similar political support analysis conducted for President George
H.W. Bush using a survey conducted during the summer of 1992 (Hibbing and Theiss-Morse 1995) found very similar patterns. Although the
study contained somewhat different questions (see appendix B for question wording), support for the first President Bush was tied largely to
party identification, race and presidential performance on the economy
(Farnsworth 1997, 2001b). In that case, of course, the Republicans were
more likely to rate the president highly and African Americans—one of
the strongest pro-Democratic voting blocs—were more likely to rate the
president negatively.

Women, who as a group also lean Democratic in their politics, were
more likely than men to favor Clinton in the 2000 survey (Table 3.2) and
to favor Bush in the 1992 survey, but neither variable achieved statistical
significance. Gender differences, in other words, were far less pronounced than racial differences for assessing these two former presidents
during their final months in office. Despite these findings relating to
assessment of incumbent presidents, women have been more likely to
support Democratic candidates for president than men in every presidential election held over the past several decades (Jackson and Crotty
2001; Wayne 2003).

In the test for generational differences in 1992, partisanship again mattered for all generational groups, as did Bush's perceived performance
in handling the top national program, which, for most people in 1992,
was the economy (Farnsworth 1997; Hibbing and Theiss-Morse 1995).
Because the survey used for 1992 contained a question that also asked
how well Congress was thought to be doing on that top problem, research revealed that overall and for the Next, Boom and Silent generational groups, the worse a job Congress was thought to do in handling
the top national problem, the higher Bush's specific support became
(Farnsworth 1997). This finding is consistent with Bush's efforts in 1991
and 1992 to criticize heavily the then–Democratically controlled Congress
in advance of his reelection campaign, a sometimes attractive strategy in
times of divided government (Corrado 1994; Hershey 1997; Mayhew
1991). After Republicans won majorities in the U.S. House and the U.S.
Senate in 1994, Bill Clinton did much the same thing, trying to sail to
reelection in 1996 by portraying the opposing party as extremist (Edwards 2000). In Clinton's case, however, this strategy worked and he
easily secured a second term (Ceaser and Busch 1997).

SUPPORT FOR CONGRESS

For all the public focus on the presidency, it is by no means clear that
the executive branch should be at the center of research involving citizen

discontent with government. Over the past decade, a number of researchers have presented a compelling case that citizen discontent may be focused far more clearly on the legislative branch than the executive branch (Asher and Barr 1994; Craig 1993; Durr, Gilmour and Wolbrecht 1997; Hibbing and Theiss-Morse 1995; Kimball and Patterson 1997; Mayer and Canon 1999).

> Congress embodies practically everything Americans dislike about politics. It is large and therefore ponderous; it operates in a presidential system and is therefore independent and powerful; it is open and therefore disputes are played out for all to see; it is based on compromise and therefore reminds people of the disturbing fact that most issues do not have right answers. Much of what the public dislikes about Congress is endemic to what a legislature is. (Hibbing and Theiss-Morse 1995:60)

Of course the idea that Congress is a broken branch of the political system is hardly a new idea. More than a generation ago, political scientists focused in on lawmakers as being short-sighted seekers of their own self-preservation (Mayhew 1974). Lawmakers were seen as being drawn increasingly to publicity rather than the hard work of crafting legislation away from the television cameras (Cook 1989). More than a decade ago, critics observed that Congress needed to be restructured to provide an improved discussion of broad policy principles rather than having Capitol Hill focus on strategic mechanisms that protect narrow constituent interests (cf., Dodd 1993).

As the Framers intended, the pressures on individual lawmakers in Congress are quite different from those pressures on a president. Individuals members of the U.S. House and the U.S. Senate do not face the same pressures either, as they run in different districts at different times. Even members of the U.S. House do not face identical pressures. Modern redistricting procedures in the states create congressional districts with little in common, and members running for reelection generally operate as individual entrepreneurs, raising their own funds and tailoring their own campaigns for local constituent consumption (Arnold 1990, Jacobson 2001). In fact, many incumbent members run for Congress as individuals by running against Congress as an institution (Craig 1993).

Some members of Congress have tried, in different ways, to improve lawmaking on Capitol Hill. From inside the Capitol, reformers like former House Speaker Newt Gingrich have sought to streamline the process (Gingrich 1995). Congressional scholars and Democratic members of Congress, however, have complained that the streamlined processes developed by the Republican Party after the 1994 election bypassed public access to the political process and thereby led to poorly crafted legislation, increased partisan bickering and greater citizen frustration (cf., Mann 1996; Cardin 1996). From inside the Capitol, reformers like Senator John McCain (R-Ariz.) have sought to reduce the influence of special interests in lawmaking (Drew 2002). But, according to its supporters, the campaign finance reform legislation championed by McCain for years and signed in 2002 by President George W. Bush subsequently was being undermined through bureaucratic interpretation (Edsall 2002; Wertheimer 2002).

Some researchers have argued that public perceptions of the apparent fairness of legislative procedures are central to understandings of public frustrations with Congress. In other words, citizens are not really angry about actual policy outcomes, rather, they are frustrated with the process of legislating (Hibbing and Theiss-Morse 1995, 1998). Along these same lines, issues of "procedural justice," that is, whether policymakers act fairly in deciding among the various policy alternatives, are thought to play major roles in citizen acceptance of policy outcomes (Tyler 1988; Tyler and Rasinski 1991).

A key way that individual lawmakers improve their chances for reelection is through the use of "particularized benefits," special gifts to one's own constituents thanks to the intervention of a lawmaker (Mayhew 1974). Indeed, many campaigns focus intensely on the delivery of legislative pork, be it a new highway, a new flood control project or a benefit for a local employer (Fenno 1992; Jacobson 2001).

Taken together, these findings suggest that political support for Congress is likely to be a matter involving far more perceived responsiveness than support for the presidency, particularly given the efforts by many legislators to convince their constituents that an important part of being a congressman or congresswoman is bringing home the district's share of legislative pork.

Generational Differences in Congressional Approval

Table 3.3 provides information on how the four different generational groups evaluated the Republican-led Congress in 2000. As was the case for the evaluations of President Clinton, the G.I. generation, the oldest generational group, had the highest percentage of respondents giving high marks in the evaluation of the legislative branch of the political system. As was the case for the presidential evaluations, the Next generation, the youngest group, had the lowest percentage of respondents giving high marks.

Evaluations of Congress, are clustered in the middle values. The evaluations in the neutral range for Congress (scores of 41–60) ranged from a low of 38 percent from the G.I. generation to a high of 52 percent of the Next generation; neutral evaluations of Clinton ranged from 20 percent of the Silent generation to 23 percent of the Next generation. This pattern may be a result of the presidency's dominance of media coverage

Table 3.3
Generations and Approval of Congress

The Congressional approval thermometer rating (0-100 scale) is condensed into five categories.

2000	NEXT	BOOM	SILENT	GI	CHI-SQUARE (signif)
81-100 HIGH	6%	8%	9%	14%	
61-80	23%	25%	29%	30%	
41-60 NEUTRAL	52%	48%	47%	38%	.04
21-40	15%	16%	14%	13%	
0-20 LOW	5%	4%	1%	4%	

of government. The White House gets far more coverage than Congress under ordinary circumstances—and President Clinton's travails were anything but ordinary (Graber 2002; Sabato, Stencel and Lichter 2000; Waterman, Wright and St. Clair 1999). Clearly, it is easy for many individuals to develop firm opinions, for or against, the first president to face impeachment proceedings in more than a century. It would be much harder to form such firm opinions for something as diverse and unwieldy as the 535-member conglomerate of the U.S. House and the U.S. Senate. This difficulty is particularly problematic given "Fenno's Paradox," in which citizens may dislike Congress as an institution but adore their own representative (Farnsworth 2003a; Fenno 1975; Hibbing and Theiss-Morse 1995). Despite all the expressed frustrations with Congress, note that no more than 5 percent of the respondents in any generational group gave Congress very low marks. Clinton received a far greater percentage of very negative evaluations, with between 17 and 24 percent of each generation group giving him a rating of 20 or below.

What Explains Public Approval of Congress?

Table 3.4 provides the OLS regression analysis that allows us to see what factors are related to how positively or negatively citizens evalu-

Table 3.4
Support for Congress and Generations: OLS Regression Analysis

2000	Unstandardized Coefficients (b)			
	ALL	NEXT	BOOM	SILENT
Education	-1.27***	-.64	-1.49*	-1.45
Income	-.05	.10	.23	-.60
Sex	2.92**	3.82*	3.69*	-1.19
White	-1.86	-2.91	-1.17	-1.03
African American	5.40*	4.41	7.03	3.57
Party ID (Unfolded)	.22	.27	-.16	1.09
Ideology (Unfolded)	1.14***	1.27*	1.08	.92
Political Trust Index	2.34***	2.49***	2.62***	1.78**
Efficacy Index	.11	.13	-.05	.23
Economy Past Year	1.26**	1.97**	.90	-.68
Economy Next Year	.67	.17	1.92*	-.98
U.S. World Position	.30	.48	-.73	1.63
Responsiveness Index	2.89***	3.25***	2.01*	.3.39**
Interpersonal Trust Index	.23*	.25	.28	-.04
Adjusted R-sq.	.18***	.20***	.17***	.14***
n	1084	405	400	207

* p < .05 ** p < .01 *** p < .001

ated Congress in 2000. As before, there is an overall equation and analyses for each of the three younger generation groups. Overall, the models work reasonably well, though they are not as effective as those designed to explain the evaluations of President Clinton (see Table 3.2).

Support for Congress depended far more on how one felt about the procedural justice issue of whether government appeared to be responsive and whether government could be trusted than on questions of performance. President Clinton was evaluated on the basis of how well he handled issues like war and peace and the economy as well as on political trust, while Congress was evaluated largely on the extent to which it was operating in an open and trustworthy manner. While economic performance did matter in the overall model, it was far less consequential for evaluations of Congress in 2000 than for evaluations of President Clinton.

Other factors of consequence in the overall Congress model (the "all" column) include ideology (in 2000 conservatives liked Congress more than liberals did), education (with the less-educated citizens expressing more favorable opinions regarding Congress) and sex (women were more positively disposed than men). Race also matters, as African Americans rated Congress more positively than other racial groups did. There is also, for the overall model, a sense that Congress was at least a distant part of one's political community: The higher one's level of interpersonal trust, the more positively one viewed Congress.

The heavy reliance on political trust and perceived responsiveness is entirely supportive of the procedural justice idea, namely, that Congress is evaluated more on the basis of how it behaves than on the basis of the policies it actually enacts. This pattern also reflects the legislative reality that whatever Congress may want to do, it is unlikely to get very far unless the president is in agreement. Without the quasi-religious aura of the Supreme Court, without the ceremony and profound emotional attachment enjoyed by the president, Congress is held to a high standard of responsiveness and trustworthiness.

A few comparisons of the competence measures contained in the 2000 evaluations of Congress and President Clinton are in order. Note the slightly higher punishment/reward dimension for a president as compared to Congress (See Tables 3.2 and 3.4). Presidents who do well by voters on key policies are rewarded to a greater degree in terms of public support than is a similarly effective Congress; conversely, presidents are punished more severely for doing poorly. This makes some intuitive sense: Finding blame and directing praise is a more complicated business on Capitol Hill than at the White House. After all, the buck does not stop at the desk of House Speaker Dennis Hastert (R-Ill.) or that of Senate Majority Leader Bill Frist (R-Tenn.). This finding also tends to square with past research that suggests citizens blame presidents more than legislators for bad economic times and credit presidents more than legislators for good economic times (Lewis-Beck and Rice 1992; Jacobson 2001).

How much of a difference is there when the party labels are reversed? Not so much, it turns out. A previous study using John R. Hibbing and Elizabeth Theiss-Morse's (1995) survey data for 1992, when Republican President George H.W. Bush faced a Democratic-controlled Congress, found very similar patterns (Farnsworth 1997, 2001b). How positively one evaluated Congress in 1992 depended largely on the same procedural justice issues: one's level of trust in the political system and the extent to which the legislative branch is thought to operate in a fair manner. One major difference in 1992, however, was the far more important role played by partisanship in evaluating the legislative branch. While Republicans were disposed far more negatively and Democrats far more positively regarding the 1992 Congress (both chambers were then controlled by that party), a citizen's partisan orientations in 2000 ceased to be of significance to their evaluations of Congress. The 1992 results may have been a period effect since Congress was in particularly ill-repute at that time because of concerted efforts by Republican activists like soon-to-be House Speaker Newt Gingrich (R-Ga.) and talk radio icons like Rush Limbaugh to attack the institution and the Democrats who then ran the House (Davis and Owen 1998; Owen 1996). The House check-kiting scandal and the Clarence Thomas–Anita Hill confrontation of those years also did little to endear lawmakers themselves to the general public (Hibbing and Theiss-Morse 1995; Mayer and Abramson 1994). In 2000, when the tables were turned on Capitol Hill, the Democrats in the minority were far less aggressive in their attacks on the Republican majority.

The search for generational differences among the evaluators of Congress in 2000 finds far less-pronounced differences by age than those seen for President Clinton. All four groups placed a heavy reliance on political trust and perceived responsiveness when they evaluated Congress. One variable that achieves statistical significance in the overall model—the interpersonal trust index—fails to be statistically significant for any of the individual generational groups.

But there are some differences. The youngest generational group was the only one to evaluate Congress based on recent performance of the national economy, perhaps because this generation was more anxious about the future than the generally more established older citizens (the Next group was also the only generational group that evaluated President Clinton using this dimension). The youngest group also was inclined more than either older generation to evaluate Congress on ideological grounds. The gender gap in evaluations of Congress found in the Next generation and among the Boomers disappeared in the older Silent generation group. This result may be because of the greater focus on gender issues during the impressionable years of these two younger generations.

In 1992, when the Democrats controlled Congress, there were some distinct differences in generational perspectives regarding the legislative branch (Farnsworth 1997). During that time of general economic dissatisfaction, all generational groups evaluated Congress in part on the health of the national economy. Issues of procedural fairness remained important for the Next, Boomers and Silent generations in 1992. For both the Boomers and the G.I. generation the perception that Congress was looking out for ordinary citizens was important in 1992. For the Next and Silent generations the belief that politicians do care what citizens think helped build political support in that earlier survey (Farnsworth 1997). Again, in 1992, partisanship was found to be more relevant to younger than older citizens in the evaluation of Congress, perhaps because of the increasing partisan combat engineered by Gingrich during the impressionable years of members of this generation. Partisanship was the only background variable to matter in any of these regressions, and then only for the two younger groups. As one would expect, Democrats rated the 1992 Congress higher than did Republicans.

A comparison of these two years shows that some matters are consistently important in the evaluation of Congress and other matters also may be important, depending on the circumstances. The procedural justice matters of perceived responsiveness and perceived fairness are consistently important, while economic matters are more important to citizens in their evaluations of Congress when the economy is performing poorly, as it was in 1992.

SUPPORT FOR THE SUPREME COURT

Last, but not least, we turn to the Supreme Court. At the outset, the most important thing to recognize about the public's views regarding the Supreme Court is that citizens learn relatively little about this political branch. The vast majority of media coverage of public governance focuses on the presidency and the Congress, and the fact that members of both of the other branches are elected rather than appointed is yet another reason why the Supreme Court gets only a tiny fraction of the coverage of Washington happenings and personalities (Graber 2002). Another reason is that both presidents and members of Congress frequently appear before television, while cameras are banned from the Supreme Court and the individual justices rarely consent to televised interviews (Davis 1994). In fact, the media coverage of the Court is so limited that a public opinion poll a few years back found that more citizens could name the members of the long-dead comedy team the Three Stooges than even three of the nine current members of the Supreme Court (Biskupic 1995). As a result of these trends in public awareness regarding the Court, researchers believe that public support for the Supreme Court remains higher than that of other political institutions at nearly all times. Researchers also believe that the public's general positive feelings regarding the Court stem more from broad, general positive feelings regarding the political system than from the Court's actual performance on issues of concern to individual citizens (Caldeira and Gibson 1992). Because the Court's legitimacy is not derived from majority citizen endorsement in an election, matters of political support are particularly important for the Court. After all, without public support, or at least public acquiescence, citizen willingness to abide by Court decisions may be lacking.

> To persist and function effectively, political institutions must continuously try to amass and husband the goodwill of the public. For the Supreme Court, public support bulks especially large; it is an uncommonly vulnerable institution. The Court lacks an electoral connection to provide legitimacy, is sometimes obliged to stand against the winds of public opinion, operates in an environment often intolerant of those in need of defense and has none of the standard political levers over people and institutions. (Caldeira and Gibson 1992:635)

One important issue that past studies of public feelings regarding the court have revealed is that of African Americans' and whites' very different assessments regarding the judicial branch. When asked about one's willingness to obey Court decisions, what seemed to matter most was one's perceived vulnerability within the political system, an area where African Americans tended to score higher than whites (Jaros and Roper 1980).

While both African Americans and whites generally view the Court quite favorably, most African Americans are less supportive of the Court than whites are (Gibson and Caldeira 1992). But there is an important generational difference among African Americans identified in past research. African Americans who entered adulthood during the era of the Warren Court (defined as those born between 1933 and 1953) remained very supportive of the Court for decades, even though they may have disagreed with some of the justices' subsequent and more conservative rulings (Gibson and Caldeira 1992).

> Among whites there is some tendency for dissatisfaction with the Court's policy outputs to translate into diminished levels of support. But, among blacks, precisely the opposite occurs. Those who are more dissatisfied with recent judicial policies are more supportive of the court as an institution. This is strong evidence of resilience of past attitudes toward the institution. (Gibson and Caldeira 1992:1138)

Generational Differences in Approval of the Supreme Court

When we turn to Table 3.5, the comparison of the evaluations of Supreme Court by various generational groups, a familiar pattern emerges. The oldest generations were the most inclined to give very high marks to the government institution, the youngest generations were likely to

Table 3.5
Generations and Approval of the Supreme Court

The Supreme Court thermometer rating (0-100 scale) is condensed into five categories.

2000	NEXT	BOOM	SILENT	GI	CHI-SQUARE (signif)
81-100 HIGH	15%	19%	26%	32%	
61-80	34%	34%	33%	29%	
41-60 NEUTRAL	42%	37%	35%	33%	.00
21-40	5%	8%	6%	7%	
0-20 LOW	4%	2%	1%	0%	

Note: Percentages may not add to 100% because of rounding.

be more neutral in their assessments. Nearly one-third of the members of the G.I. generation, the oldest group, gave the Court a rating of 81 or higher, more than twice the percentage of the members of the youngest generation. Very, very few people gave the Court a score of 20 or below; all generation groups were positively disposed to the judicial branch.

When we compare the year 2000 thermometer evaluations for President Clinton, the Congress and the Supreme Court, it is clear that familiarity can breed both contempt and affection. President Clinton was viewed negatively by a much larger percentage of citizens of all generation groups than the members of the legislative or judicial branches, but he was viewed more positively than the Congress and about as positively as the Court, despite a very controversial presidential tenure. While most citizens gave neutral or slightly above neutral evaluations to both Congress and the Court, there were many fewer fence-sitters regarding Bill Clinton.

What Explains Public Approval of the Supreme Court?

Table 3.6 demonstrates that the OLS regression analyses designed to explain why citizens evaluate the Supreme Court are far weaker than

Table 3.6
Support for the Supreme Court and Generations: OLS Regression Analysis

2000	Unstandardized Coefficients (b)			
	ALL	NEXT	BOOM	SILENT
Education	.30	1.83**	-.09	-.38
Income	.16	-.05	.24	.34
Sex	.24	.96	-.12	-.67
White	-.48	-.15	-.62	-3.10
African American	-.20	.43	1.74	-5.20
Party ID	-.29	.08	-.27	01
Ideology	1.04**	1.42*	.65	-.84
Political Trust Index	1.58***	1.20*	2.29***	.34
Efficacy Index	-.15	-.02	-.64	.71
Economy Past Year	.28	1.13	-.48	-1.03
Economy Next Year	.86	.10	1.44	1.04
U.S. World Position	.08	.48	-.36	.12
Responsiveness Index	2.87***	3.18***	3.29***	1.44
Interpersonal Trust Index	.05	.05	.03	-.03
Adjusted R-sq.	.07***	.09***	.08***	.00
n	1078	408	399	199

* p < .05 ** p < .01 *** p < .001

those used to evaluate the other two branches. The overall adjusted r-square, .07, is less than half of the .18 measure for the overall evaluation of Congress and a fraction of the .51 adjusted r-square for the overall evaluation of President Clinton. Clearly, the issues that tie evaluations of some political figures to citizens do not work equally well for all three of our system's branches.

Two important measures in the analysis of congressional approval were also relevant to approval of the Supreme Court: a citizen's level of political trust and the extent to which a citizen believed that government was responsive to public concerns. Ideology was also important in the overall model, with more conservatives viewing the Court favorably than liberals. None of the other background measures were significant, evidence that Americans have very similar views about the Court, regardless of whether they are rich or poor, male or female, African American or White. Neither were the government's performance on the issues of the economy and America's position in the world significant to public evaluations of the Court, as they should not be, since the other two branches are far more influential in these areas, and since these issues rarely are adjudicated (O'Brien 2000).

Members of the Silent generation, the oldest generation analyzed in Table 3.6, evaluated the Court in a very consistent fashion. Not a single variable helps us predict with any statistical significance one's evaluation of the Court. The fact that there is no difference found for race, income, education, trust in government, interpersonal trust, political efficacy or any other measure used in this analysis is further evidence of the consistently high level of respect accorded to political institutions by the members of this generation.

Younger generations, though, were more divided in their perspectives of the Court. For both the Next generation and the Boomers, issues of political trust and governmental responsiveness were relevant to evaluations of the justices. Ideology also mattered for the youngest generation group, but not for the two older generations.

A similar study of public opinion regarding the Supreme Court in 1992 provided similar results. That Court, which also had a conservative majority, was regarded positively by most citizens in all age groups (Farnsworth 1997). Using the survey fielded by political scientists Hibbing and Theiss-Morse (1995), an earlier analysis found that evaluations of the Supreme Court in 1992 were based largely on the Court's perceived fairness (Farnsworth 1997). There were both racial and age gaps, however. In 1992, the younger one was, the more one tended to support the Court. The Court's more controversial rulings in the past—decisions involving desegregation, abortion, school busing, increasing national power and expanding the rights of criminal defendants—are all part of the lives of older Americans, while the Court in the lifetime of younger Americans has been far less controversial, *Bush v. Gore* excepted. The Supreme Court of forty or even thirty years ago was far more willing to try to settle divisive issues in controversial ways than is today's Court (Horowitz 1977; O'Brien 2000). Middle-aged people might have been more inclined to remember pitched battles over such things as civil rights and the protection of criminal defendants during their impressionable years, while younger people might have been more likely to consider the less activist and generally less controversial Burger and Rehnquist Courts in their evaluations.

African Americans might have been frustrated with the Supreme Court of 1992 for this same reason—the Court has stepped away from some of its more aggressive remedies to counter discrimination in employment, education and the enforcement of criminal justice (O'Brien 2000). Similarly, African Americans may have become more negatively disposed toward the Court after Clarence Thomas, a Republican African American opposed to affirmative action, replaced Thurgood Marshall, a Democratic African American who played a central role in support of desegregation as a civil rights lawyer and later as a justice on the Supreme Court (Merida and Fletcher 2002; O'Brien 2000). But the passage of time may have healed some wounds; by the time of the 2000 survey, there was no racial gap in evaluations of the Court, which continues to contain Clarence Thomas and the four other conservative justices who sat on the Court at the time of the 1992 survey. The two newest justices on the Court at the time of this writing, Stephen Breyer and Ruth Bader Ginsburg, are part of the Court's liberal minority and joined the Court during Clinton's first term.

In 1992, a similar model was also far less able to explain support for the Supreme Court than for the other parts of the political system. The 1992 analysis was best at predicting support for the youngest cohort, as was the case with the 2000 survey. The perceived fairness of government policies was an issue for both the Next generation and the Silent generation in 1992, while in 2000 such issues mattered for the Next generation and the Boomers.

Why might the evaluations of the Silent generation have been so difficult to predict under this model? Well, the impressionable-years perspective has an answer. Many of the members of the Silent generation passed through their impressionable years during an era of relative peace for the Court: The oldest members of this generation were children when President Franklin Roosevelt did battle with the Court over the New Deal, and the many already would have been over 21 years of age before the landmark 1954 ruling in *Brown v. Board of Education, Topeka*. The controversies over desegregation, civil rights, abortion and free speech during the Vietnam War years, matters that repeatedly ended up before the Court, all came later (Delli Carpini 1986; O'Brien 2000). Without large numbers of divisive judicial decisions during their formative years, members of the Silent generation would have had little reason to pay much attention to the Court, and it is close public attention, as we have seen with the case of Bill Clinton, that is essential for the creation of strongly held positive or negative feelings. While this generation is the most positive regarding the Court, the evidence shows these high evaluations are not based on any of the substantive matters examined here: For this older group, support for the Court is not based on governmental responsiveness, political trust, demographics or even ideological orientation. This generic support is very useful for a political system. Younger citizens, however, rate the Court according to a variety of substantive matters.

Taken together, the results in both 2000 and in 1992 demonstrate clear generational differences regarding an assessment of our political system, both in the abstract and in practice. The above findings have presented strong similarities in views between the two youngest generational groups on the one hand and the two oldest generational groups on the other. Much of the above discussion has focused on the Next generation, and what we have found is a study in extremes. If there are significant generational differences, the Next generation is likely to be on the edge and usually the least likely to offer very positive assessments.

CONCLUSION

Citizens approach the three branches of the U.S. political system in different ways. Likewise, citizens of different ages focus on different things as they evaluate the different parts of government. The matters that are of particular concern to these generations can often be explained through distinct generational experiences. Events that occurred during the impressionable years of each generational group have influences that stretch across years, even decades. The Silent generation, reared in times of far less criticism of government than has been the norm in this country since the 1960s, consistently evaluates every part of the political system with a far more generous standard than that of younger citizens.

Among the variables used here one might note two powerful patterns: the overwhelming focus on competence in presidential evaluations and the importance of system trust and governmental responsiveness measures for evaluations of the legislative and judicial branches.

There are also some other findings of particular note. The views of African Americans in 2000 were far more similar to views of whites than they were in the 1992 survey (Farnsworth 1997). Given that 1992 marked the end of twelve years of Republican rule in the White House and that the 1992 Supreme Court consisted primarily of Republican appointees, the frustrations of many African Americans may be understandable. Given that 2000 marked the end of eight years of a Clinton presidency that often offered support for many African American policy concerns, the higher evaluations Clinton received from African Americans is likewise understandable (Sapiro and Canon 2000). The difference in evaluations of nearly the same Supreme Court in 1992 and 2000 is strange: Perhaps African Americans were particularly incensed by the replacement of Thurgood Marshall with Clarence Thomas in 1992. Eight years later, perhaps, the anger had moderated with the passage of time. Likewise, the changes between the Warren Court years and the Burger Court were more pronounced than the changes between the Burger Court and Rehnquist Court (O'Brien 2000). The passage of time also might have led to this reduction in the distinctiveness of evaluations of this branch of the federal government by African Americans.

These generational cleavages, which appear strongly in the Hibbing and Theiss-Morse (1995) measures, may indicate early cracks in the political system's reservoir of citizen support. If these cracks widen into fissures, the U.S. government may have problems in maintaining adequate political support to run the government effectively. Declining participation and with it declining legitimacy may result from declining political support (Cappella and Jamieson 1997). Such developments could make the government's job much harder, regardless of whether the country is facing times of peace and prosperity or war and economic decline.

But one should not overstate the diffuse support concerns raised by the analyses of the past two chapters. On a broader level, one can observe that the overall state of diffuse support and specific support is not completely negative, according to these results. The level of alienation detected in this study is not all that large in many cases; most people in all generations are disposed favorably toward the political system, both in its abstract and in its concrete dimensions. Citizens have expressed a great deal of frustration with government in recent years, and the results here suggest that frustrations are widespread and found in key groups. But, at the same time, there is no indication that any of these generational cohorts are totally disenchanted. This is good news for people concerned about the possibility of declining legitimation for Americans' constitutional order. Things may not be as bad as some had thought.

Nevertheless, there are signs of serious trouble on the horizon. The youngest generation consistently has been getting disposed more negatively toward the government over time, and the youthful idealism gap that was previously much in evidence for some measures in 1988 had pretty much disappeared by 2000. On some measures, the youngest citizens already have become the most cynical. Members of the Baby Boom generation have taken over much of the national political scene from their elders, and they tend to be most like the youngest group in their negativity on some issues. The groups whose members were most patriotic, those most satisfied with the democratic system and with the federal government, are exactly those whose generations are becoming progressively less influential and less numerous with the passage of time. This is not an auspicious trend from the perspective of public support for government.

The areas most important to younger generations in determining their political support tend to be precisely those areas where the government has not been doing so well lately—instilling trust in officeholders, pride in the branches of government and a belief in the fairness of outcomes. These are likely to be the key areas that will affect political support in the years ahead as well. While economic performance may help secure political support in financially flush times, today's public demands of government call for exacting standards that a government mired in disputes like Enron and Whitewater, corporate corruption, special interests and partisan gridlock seems ill equipped to provide (Craig 1993; Inglehart 1990; Jackson 1997). The passage of time also works to crystallize the negative opinions of the young, making their views a largely permanent part of the political landscape. Improving government performance on these matters promptly can still affect the younger and more impressionable members of this youngest generation, but many of them already may have developed the attitudes toward politics and government that they are likely to keep for life.

Generalization is an inexact business, and in this case predictions are made doubly difficult by the relative paucity of useful over-time data to deal with generational differences regarding political support. The relatively brief interval in which there are responses to some of these questions makes it difficult to predict the future trajectory of these measures of political support. More years are needed for clearer patterns to emerge, but this analysis gives us some insight into what seems to matter the most for maintaining and perhaps building political support among these various generational groups. In particular, it seems that the most important issues of one's impressionable years are the ones that frame a citizen's evaluation of the world of government and politics, largely for life. This chapter gives considerable grounds for concern, few reasons for hope and a clear understanding of where government is most likely to be judged by citizens as they consider their own attachments to the U.S. political system in the years ahead.

4

"The Great Destroyer?": Political Support and the Mass Media

The roles the mass media play in building, maintaining and perhaps undermining public support for political regimes and officeholders have been among the most controversial debates in political science. Throughout the twentieth century, political scientists studying media effects have gone from one extreme to the other: starting with the "hypodermic-effects" model developed to explain the success of Hitler, then shifting rapidly to the "minimal-effects" approach that was popular beginning in the late 1940s and, more recently, turning to the "media-effects" perspective that rose in response to the influence thought to be exercised by the mass media—especially television—in setting the political agenda of the 1960s and beyond.

This chapter will broaden this study of political support by focusing on the effects of the mass media—and especially television—upon citizens' emotional attachments to government and politics. At the outset, one should note that there is little agreement among political scientists about the forms these media influences actually take. Do mass media outlets undermine public attachments to government through their trivialization of news and their growing skepticism of government officials, as many recent scholars have argued (cf., Bennett 2001; Cappella and Jamieson 1997; Neuman 1986; Postman 1985; Putnam 2000; Sabato 1993)? Or do the mass media help maintain political support by providing needed political information to assist citizens in making their evaluations of government and politics efficiently (cf., Graber 1988; Page and Shapiro 1992; Popkin 1991)? Or does this alleged media enhancement of support take the shape of excluding and therefore marginalizing the more critical voices outside the power structure, as still other scholars have alleged (cf., Gitlin 1980; Ginsberg 1986; Iyengar and Kinder 1987)? These are among the issues to be worked through in this chapter.

MEDIA USE AND POLITICAL SUPPORT: TRADITIONAL VIEWS

For the generation of political scientists practicing in the 1930s and 1940s, Hitler's rapid rise to absolute power in Germany represented a terrifying nightmare crying out for explanation. How could ordinary people—citizens of one of the most educated nations on Earth—fall so rapidly and so deeply under the spell of such a man? The answer, according to many scholars of the day, was found in no small part in the content of the mass media. Hitler was able to use the new national medium of radio to broadcast his strident messages across Germany and later across Europe, and Nazi propaganda films helped build the religious fervor that pushed the Nazi movement toward worldwide destruction (cf., Nimmo and Combs 1980). Other events of the 1930s, most notably the panic that followed the "War of the Worlds" radio broadcast in the United States, also suggested great media influence, perhaps analogous to the direct influence of a hypodermic injection (Cantril 1940).

Studies of vote choice, however, indicated that media impacts were not very strong. In particular, media content did not appear to affect vote choice (Lazarsfeld, Berelson and Gaudet 1948). At most, media influence was indirect, taking place through a two-step communication process in which opinion leaders (e.g., union leaders, more educated relatives or other respected members of a peer group) passed media messages on to other citizens. This perspective, supported by additional research that undermined the hypodermic effects model, did little to encourage the study of media effects in this era (Cook 1998). Research in political socialization, which began in earnest during this period, regarded the news media as far less important than the "primary" political socialization agents of family, school and peers (Dawson and Prewitt 1969). The main role played by the media, this line of thinking went, is to reenforce previously held opinions, as individuals selectively remembered the information that was consistent with their existing personal views and prejudices (Klapper 1960).

The greatest change was the mass availability of television during the 1950s. Television had the potential for being far more influential than print for a variety of reasons: (1) It offered an expanded range of information—both moving pictures and words, (2) it offered the potential for being more credible ("Seeing Is Believing," as the saying goes) and (3) television rapidly became ubiquitous in American households—a main source of information and entertainment (cf., Grossman 1995; Ranney 1983; White 1961). The key events of American politics in the 1960s—the civil rights movement, the Vietnam War, the space race and the assassinations of John F. Kennedy, Robert F. Kennedy and Martin Luther King Jr.—and their aftermaths lent themselves to powerful (and emotion-invoking) visual images (Grossman 1995; Halberstam 1979; Lesher 1982;

McGinniss 1969; Meyrowitz 1985; White 1978). So, too, did the 1960 presidential election, the first to include nationally televised debates—con-
frontations that pitted the sunny features of a media-savvy Jack Kennedy
against the pale-complexioned and otherwise unattractive visage of Richard Nixon (Perret 2001; White 1961).

These events, evidence of the considerable influence of television,
forced a rethinking of the minimal-effects media influence paradigm. By
the late 1970s, media scholars settled on the idea that media effects could
be substantial, particularly in the areas of setting the agenda and framing
the debate (McCombs and Shaw 1977; Robinson 1976; Iyengar 1991; Iyengar and Kinder 1987). Political scientist Thomas E. Patterson (1980) found
evidence during presidential elections of a "bandwagon" effect, in which
reporters created candidate momentum through coverage patterns. Michael J. Robinson and Margaret A. Sheehan (1983) found that television
coverage was growing more distinct, and ever more trivial, with its con-
centration on horse-race standings rather than on substantive issues. Subsequent research has found this trend has intensified as the years have
passed (Farnsworth and Lichter 2003).

While there is a general consensus among media scholars concerning
the validity of the "more than minimal" perspective on media effects,
today's media debates contest fiercely the results of media influence,
particularly regarding the public's emotional connections to government
and politics. Some scholars argue that the primary impact of today's
media environment is to increase citizen cynicism, while others insist
that current coverage distracts citizens, making it easier for political elites
to do what they want to do away from public scrutiny.

MEDIA USE AND POLITICAL SUPPORT: CURRENT PERSPECTIVES

The recent debates over media influence start from a point of general
agreement: Today's television and newspaper stories about government
are far more negative than in the past (cf., Farnsworth and Lichter 2003;
Kerbel 1995; Patterson 1993; Sabato 1993). Where scholars disagree, and
disagree strongly, is over what this increased negativity means for American government and politics. A key problem has been an inability to
demonstrate consistently that media impacts are as powerful (and, one
might add, as destructive) as many scholars expect (cf., Bartels 1993).

One strong current of research has developed under the concept of
"media malaise," that media exposure can increase citizen cynicism and
negativity (Robinson 1976). The steady drumbeat of negative coverage,
this theory holds, leads to increased numbers of citizens "tuning out"
from government and politics (Capella and Jamieson 1997; Putnam 2000).
The news media, and television in particular, stand accused of contrib-
uting to a fragmentary, haphazard public understanding of issues

through their generally entertainment-oriented (and superficial) coverage (Farnsworth and Lichter 2003; Kerbel 1995, 1998; Neuman 1986; Patterson 1993; Postman 1985; Sabato 1993).

Political scientist Roderick P. Hart (1994) expanded on this observation by suggesting that people may feel like they are participating in politics solely by the act of consuming media. Researchers argue that television misinforms the public and teaches us that politics is not all that complicated and, in fact, is not worth much respect. "We tower above politics by making it seem beneath us," Hart wrote (1994:8). But this erroneous public impression of politics as some form of gossip is dangerous, he observed. Democracy is "imperiled (1) when its people do not know what they think they know and (2) when they do not care about what they do not know. Television miseducates the citizenry, but worse, it makes that miseducation attractive" (Hart 1994:12).

Of course, television news is not monolithic. Although the Big Three networks often provide very similar fare, cable and satellite television offer a wide variety of news and information sources, some of which can be quite different in content and perspective than the work of ABC, CBS and NBC (Farnsworth and Lichter 2003). Variety, great variety in fact, also can be found through perusing the new media sources available on the Internet (Drudge 2000; Hall 2001; Seib 2001).

While the Internet is a rapidly expanding medium, its influence remains more limited than many technologically savvy young adults might think. A survey conducted shortly after the highly interesting 2000 presidential election found that 66 percent of Americans never went online for election news, and an additional 17 percent only went online twice a week or less (Pew 2000b). Only 10 percent of those surveyed said they went online at least once a day during the election period for political news. In contrast, nearly 29 percent of those surveyed in the 2000 ANES said they watched the evening news every night, and 34 percent of those surveyed said they read a newspaper every day. The Internet may someday revolutionize politics, as some of its supporters may hope, but the relatively small number of people going online regularly during the 2000 election suggests that such predictions have not yet come true (Farnsworth and Owen 2001). For that election, public attention remained focused on television, which 70 percent say was one of their leading sources of news and information, and on newspapers, which was a leading source of election information for 39 percent (Pew 2000a). The Internet was a leading source for only 11 percent, that survey found. (Because people could give up to two responses, the figures from the survey conducted by the Pew Research Center for the People and the Press exceed 100 percent.) Television, in other words, remains the leading source for citizens seeking information about government, though its audience has been declining over the past decade (Kurtz 2002).

Throughout this project we have identified major differences between the way citizens view the political system as a whole (diffuse support) and the way citizens evaluate the individuals leading the component branches of that political system (specific support). Since television is far more likely to concentrate on specific personalities than on issues, much less the adequacy of the American political system, negative reports may not lead to a weakening of the political system, though they may prove disadvantageous for individual politicians caught in the scandal coverage (cf., Bennett 2001).

> For most men most of the time, politics is a series of pictures in the mind, placed there by television news, newspapers, magazines, discussions. The pictures create a moving panorama taking place in a world the mass public never quite touches, yet one its members come to fear or cheer, often with passion and sometimes with action. (Edelman 1985:5; cf., Lippmann 1965 [1922])

The process through which citizens process these pictures may be a very complicated one. Indeed, critical coverage of specific issues does not have to undermine the political system, as was the case for television news coverage of the Vietnam War—easily one of this country's most divisive issues since the invention of that medium (Hallin 1984).

Some researchers go even further and suggest that media effects actually add up to system-building activities, even as reporters may criticize individual politicians. Television and newspapers can act as "boundary-maintaining" institutions that declare certain types of criticism too threatening for mass dissemination. Television may mold the views of the mass public to reflect elite values; media polls may help make opinion expression more docile, according to some researchers (Ginsberg 1986). These polls likewise can give government leaders the information they need to manipulate public sentiment effectively (Ginsberg 1986). While these conclusions clearly are not prescriptions for responsive government, they do not suggest the evaporation of mass support for the political system either (cf., Iyengar and Kinder 1987).

> Television news may be objective, but it is far from neutral. The production of news takes place within boundaries established by official sources and dominant values. . . . We see television news as inherently a cautious and conservative medium, much more likely to defend traditional values and institutions than attack them. (Iyengar and Kinder 1987:133)

Along these same lines, the agenda-setting and priming influences suggest that coverage of government and elections can lead to increased citizen interest in politics and government (cf., Iyengar and Kinder 1987; McCombs and Shaw 1977; Owen 1991). Indeed, people made angry by what is on television and in the newspapers may be very likely to care about government, given the increased salience resulting from a negative reaction to that information (cf., Downs 1957).

Some scholars think some branches of the government may be treated more negatively than others. Political scientist Robinson (1981) believed that very sophisticated messages regarding political support may be communicated through the mass media. While the media may help or hurt individual politicians, television news and newspapers also can be very be hard on institutions, particularly Congress.

> The media, by focusing so fully on the office of the president and then inevitably on the inadequacies of any person holding the job, may be producing an office that is more powerful but at the same time may be weakening the political power of each individual president. On the other hand, by treating Congress poorly but its incumbents relatively well, the media may be strengthening incumbents but weakening their institution. This has probably been at work since the advent of national radio. (Robinson 1981:92–93)

But the different branches of the political system are not the only divisions worth considering as we analyze the impact of the mass media on political support. Many of the scholars above have reached different conclusions concerning television and newspapers, suggesting that separate analyses are appropriate for these media sources.

In one of the more extensive studies of this issue, political scientists Diana Owen and Jack Dennis (1990) found that television viewing may help build political support. Using a model that included a number of statistical controls to separate out the impact of many key demographic and political factors, they concluded that television use enhances political support, though newspaper use appeared to undermine political support. Another researcher considering such differences found that newspaper and magazine reading have a far greater effect upon an individual's participation in politics than does television watching, but discovered the effect concentrated more in increasing political interest than in direct electoral participation like voting (Olsen 1982:87). Perhaps some form of social mobilization is at work here: The more one learns about politics, the more one is brought into politics and the more one chooses to participate in politics (Olsen 1982).

WHO WATCHES AND READS THE NEWS?

The 2000 ANES asked those surveyed how often they watched network news and how often they read a newspaper, the two media sources considered here. More than a quarter of those surveyed (26.8 percent) said they never watched network news, while a slightly larger number (28.5 percent) said they watched the network newscasts every day. A total of 30.2 percent said they watched the news between one and three days a week, and 14.5 percent said they watched network news four to six days a week.

The percentages were very similar for newspaper readership. Just over a quarter of those surveyed (25.9 percent) said they never read a newspaper, while 33.8 percent said they read a newspaper every day. A total of 29.2 percent said they read a paper one to three days a week, and 11.1 percent said they read a paper four to six days a week.

But these general readership patterns obscure substantial generational differences in viewership and readership. Table 4.1 shows that in 2000 older citizens were far more likely to watch television news every day than younger citizens: sixty-two percent of the G.I. generation, the oldest group, said they watched television news every day, more than four times the 14 percent of the members of the youngest generation group, the Next generation, who watched television news every day. More than one-third (36 percent) of the members of the youngest generation said they never watched television news, as compared to 16 percent of the G.I. generation, 15 percent of the Silent generation and 26 percent of the members of the Baby Boom generation.

The youngest generation group was also far less interested in reading a daily newspaper. Exactly one-third (33 percent) of the youngest group said they never read a paper, as compared to 23 percent of the Boomers and 20 percent of both of the two oldest generation groups. A total of 63 percent of the G.I. generation members said they read a newspaper every day, as compared to 55 percent of the Silent generation, 32 percent of the Boomers and 19 percent of the Next generation. The chi-square tests demonstrate that the generational differences in both television news watching and newspaper reading are statistically significant.

If television news is as destructive to political support as some researchers have argued, this trend may turn out to be, in a perverse way, good news. If the content of television news makes citizens more cynical, then not watching television news may be good a thing. (This is not a recommended approach, of course. If watching the television news makes one view government more negatively, then not watching may make one more less negatively disposed to government. But it would make one less informed as well, hardly an ideal outcome from the point of view of responsible citizenship.) Of course, the youngest citizens are more likely to get their news from the Internet than some of their more technologically challenged elders. While there is not much research yet on the question of how Internet content compares to that of mainstream media, some preliminary studies suggest that candidate-sponsored Internet content is more informative and substantive than the campaign

Table 4.1
Generational Differences in Use of Newspapers and Television

Television 2000	NEXT	BOOM	SILENT	GI	CHI-SQUARE (signif)
7 Days	14%	28%	47%	62%	
4-6 Days	12%	19%	16%	7%	.00
1-3 Days	39%	28%	22%	15%	
0 Days	36%	26%	15%	16%	

Newspaper 2000	NEXT	BOOM	SILENT	GI	CHI-SQUARE (signif)
7 Days	19%	32%	55%	63%	
4-6 Days	12%	13%	10%	6%	.00
1-3 Days	36%	32%	15%	11%	
0 Days	33%	23%	20%	20%	

Note: Percentages may not add to 100% because of rounding.

information provided on television network newscasts (Farnsworth and Lichter 2003).

NEWSPAPER AND TELEVISION USE: EFFECTS ON POLITICAL SUPPORT

Media Use and Approval of the Political System Overall

This next section searches for effects of television viewership and newspaper readership upon political support by analyzing the responses

Table 4.2
Media Use and Democratic Satisfaction Rating

Television 2000	0 Days	1-3 Days	4-6 Days	7 Days	CHI-SQUARE (signif)
4 HIGH	30%	29%	29%	40%	
3	45%	53%	54%	45%	
2	19%	16%	15%	11%	.00
1 LOW	7%	3%	3%	4%	

Newspaper 2000	0 Days	1-3 Days	4-6 Days	7 Days	CHI-SQUARE (signif)
4 HIGH	30%	29%	32%	36%	
3	46%	50%	53%	48%	
2	20%	15%	14%	12%	.01
1 LOW	5%	6%	1%	4%	

Note: Percentages may not add to 100% because of rounding.

to a variety of questions from the 2000 ANES, questions that we have been using throughout the previous chapters. We look at democratic satisfaction, as well as evaluations of President Clinton, Congress and the Supreme Court. First, though, we consider the central issue of democratic satisfaction. Do people who watch a lot of television news feel a lot more negatively about this country than those who do not? Do people who regularly read their newspaper have greater hostility to the political system than those who do not read the paper? The answer is found in Table 4.2.

With respect to television news viewers, we see that the more days a week a person watched news, the more satisfied that person was with American democracy. Four out of ten people who watched television news every day gave democracy the highest possible score, and another 45 percent gave it the second highest score. Only four percent of the high media users gave democracy the lowest possible score—and this in the wake of the most controversial presidential election in a century! While all groups were quite positive—about three quarters of each television viewership group gave American democracy the highest or second highest possible score—those watching the least amount of television news were the most negative. Just over one-quarter (26 percent) of those who never watched television news gave democracy the lowest or second lowest score, as compared to 19 percent of those watching the news one, two or three days a week, 18 percent of those watching network news four, five and six days a week and 15 percent of those watching television news seven days a week. The pattern here is clear (and statistically significant): The more television news one watched, the more likely one was to rate American democracy highly.

The same is true for newspaper readership in 2000: The more days a week one paid attention to news, the more positively one evaluated American democracy. Although the pattern is not as pronounced as for television news watchers, the pattern is still statistically significant. More than one third (36 percent) of those who read a paper every day gave American democracy the highest possible score, above the 29 percent, 30 percent and 32 percent recorded by the three other viewership groups. The people who didn't read the paper were the most negative: twenty-five percent of them gave American democracy low scores (40 or below), as compared to 21 percent of those who read the paper one to three days a week, the 15 percent who read the paper four to six days a week and the 16 percent who read the paper every day. Again, the 2000 ANES provides very clear results: The most positive evaluations of American democracy come from the people who read the newspaper often. The most negative evaluations came from citizens who never read the paper, or looked at it only rarely.

The results here refute the arguments made by some media scholars that newspapers and televisions are undermining public support for American democracy. In fact, the opposite is true. The greater one's consumption of newspaper and television news, the more positively one evaluates American democracy. Even if the content of the media messages are critical of government—and the evidence suggests the coverage often is negative—the negativity does not appear to affect citizen orientations to the government overall. Perhaps the effect will be seen most clearly in subsequent sections of the chapter, when we consider media use patterns and the levels of support expressed for the three branches of government.

The 2000 ANES also allows us to compare those people who relied mostly on television news with those who relied mostly on newspapers. When one compares the responses to the two media use questions, we can create three groups of media consumers: those who watched the television news more often than they read a newspaper, those who read the newspaper more than they watched television news and those who used both media sources for the same number of days per week. Nearly four out of every ten surveyed in this 2000 poll read the newspapers more days than they watched television news (38.9 percent to be exact), while 33.3 percent watched television news more and 27.8 percent used both media sources equally. We can then compare these groups to see if one media user profile is more likely to be disposed negatively toward government than the other two.

In fact, the comparisons failed to achieve statistical significance and so will be discussed in the text only briefly (and not presented in a data table). Of the television-dominant media consumers, 3.8 percent gave democracy the lowest score, as did 3.8 percent of the newspaper-dominant media consumers. For those who relied on both media forms equally, 4.8 percent gave American democracy the lowest score. These are trivial differences, to be sure.

Little needs to be said about differences this small. One only needs to note that neither media outlet seems to be a powerful force for generating cynicism when citizens evaluate the overall political system. The results for each of the three media use profiles in 2000 are almost identical.

The 1996 ANES allowed for the creation of similar groups of news consumers. Four years earlier, the newspaper-dominant group included 38 percent of the respondents, the television-dominant group contained 40 percent of those participating in the survey and the remaining 22 percent were in the mixed group. As in 2000, the comparisons among these three groups on the question of democratic satisfaction did not achieve statistical significance. Two percent of the newspaper-dominant media consumers gave American democracy the lowest score, as did 2 percent of the mixed group. The television group was slightly higher, with 3 percent, but, again, the differences among the three groups were insignificant.

Much clearer differences were found in 1996 for media use comparisons involving the federal government thermometer evaluation, in which people rated the national government on a scale with a low of zero and a high of 100 (cf., Farnsworth 1997). Twelve percent of the mixed media group gave the federal government a score of 81 or higher, as compared to 11 percent of news consumers who focused on television and 7 percent who focused on newspapers. When one considers only those in the clearly positive range of this evaluation (above 60), the television-dominant group became the most optimistic: thirty-one percent of television viewers gave scores of 61 or above, as compared to 30 percent of the mixed group and 22 percent of the newspaper-dominant media consumers. These differences are statistically significant.

Other similar tests were not so successful. A similar test of the federal government thermometer question in the 2000 ANES failed to achieve statistically significant differences for these media groups. A parallel examination of political support using the 1992 survey conducted by John R. Hibbing and Elizabeth Theiss-Morse (1995) found no statistically significant differences in political support overall on the part of the different media consumption groups (Farnsworth 1997).

Taken together, these various comparisons across the past three presidential election cycles demonstrate that the indictment sometimes made against the news media for undermining democracy appears to fail for lack of evidence (cf., Norris 2000). In fact, it would be easier to build a case that greater media use is part of the process of building greater political support. In many cases here, higher levels of television news use and newspaper use actually increase positive feelings toward government: The more news one watches or reads, the more positively one feels about the political system. The most negative citizens are found among those who rarely or never consume news on television and in the newspapers, at least in those cases where there are statistically significant differences. Along the same lines, the 2000 ANES failed to generate statistically significant differences among those who were television-dominant news consumers, newspaper-dominant news consumers and those who used both media. A survey four years earlier showed some significant differences, with television-dominant news consumers a bit more positively disposed than newspaper readers (Farnsworth 1997).

Media Use and Approval of President Clinton

Table 4.3 addresses the question of whether people who watched a lot of television news felt more negatively about President Clinton than those who did not. Contrary to what one may expect, given the massive coverage of the Clinton-Lewinsky scandal and of the president's subsequent impeachment trial, a familiar pattern emerges: The greatest percentage of those citizens giving Clinton the highest score are found in the group that watched the most television news. Of those who watched the network news every day, 28 percent of those surveyed in 2000 gave Clinton a score of 81 or higher, as compared to 22 percent of those watching television news four to six days of a week, 18 percent of those watching one to three days and 15 percent of those who did not watch television news. These differences, based on the amount of television use, are highly statistically significant.

Table 4.3
Television Use and Evaluations of Bill Clinton

Television 2000	0 Days	1-3 Days	4-6 Days	7 Days	CHI-SQUARE (signif)
81-100 HIGH	15%	18%	22%	28%	
61-80	23%	25%	26%	20%	
41-60 NEUTRAL	29%	22%	17%	18%	.00
21-40	14%	18%	17%	14%	
0-20 LOW	20%	18%	19%	20%	

Notes: Differences in the evaluation of Clinton among newspaper readers failed to achieve statistical significance (chi-square significance = .27).

Percentages may not add to 100% because of rounding.

Dividing the 2000 respondents into the three media groups discussed above—those who relied mostly on television news, mostly on newspapers and equally on both—shows that newspaper-dominant news consumers were the least likely to give Clinton an 81-point score or higher (results not shown). Only 16 percent of those using mostly newspapers gave Clinton high marks, as compared to 25 percent of those using mostly television and 22 percent in the group that used both media sources equally. Even though all three groups were almost equally likely to give Clinton a score of 20 or lower (the percentages range from 18.8 percent to 19.6 percent for the three groups), the overall differences for these three groups achieved statistical significance.

Other models show similar patterns. Using the same thermometer evaluation of Bill Clinton but replacing amount of television use with amount of newspaper use fails to generate statistically significant differences in 2000. A 1992 study comparing the evaluations of then President George H.W. Bush from among the members of the three media profiles—those who relied mostly on newspapers, mostly on television and equally on the two—also found no statistically significant differences among the different media use groups (Farnsworth 1997).

Table 4.4
Television Use and Evaluations of Congress

Television 2000	0 Days	1-3 Days	4-6 Days	7 Days	CHI-SQUARE (signif)
81-100 HIGH	6%	8%	9%	9%	
61-80	21%	25%	27%	29%	
41-60 NEUTRAL	55%	50%	43%	43%	.10 (not significant)
21-40	13%	14%	18%	15%	
0-20 LOW	5%	3%	4%	3%	

Notes: Differences in the evaluation of Congress among newspapers readers failed to achieve statistical significance (chi-square significance = .44).

Percentages may not add to 100% because of rounding.

Media Use and Approval of Congress

Table 4.4 presents evidence on the question of how television use affects approval of Congress. Here, the most frequent users of television news were most likely to give high marks to Congress and those who watched no television news were the least likely to do so. The reverse is also true: The nonwatchers were most likely to give Congress a very low score (20 or lower). But the results in Table 4.4 are not pronounced enough to reach an acceptable level of statistical significance (the chi-square significance should be .05 or less, here it is .10). There was an even weaker performance when the amount of newspaper use was used to search for differences in the evaluations of Congress, and so those results are not shown in Table 4.4.

The pattern of nonfindings for media use and approval of Congress continues when we search for differences by media user, as television-dominant news consumers, print-dominant news consumers and those who used both media formats equally had very similar patterns regarding their 2000 assessments of Congress (results not shown). A study using similar measures from a 1992 survey (Hibbing and Theiss-Morse 1995), likewise found no statistically significant differences in the evaluation of that institution, then under Democratic control, among the various media use groups (Farnsworth 1997). The lack of findings occurred despite the intense scandal coverage of those years, a period marked by the House banking scandal and by the Senate's handling of Anita Hill's allegations against Clarence Thomas (Hibbing and Theiss-Morse 1995; Mayer and Abramson 1994).

Media Use and Approval of the Supreme Court

Table 4.5 provides evidence regarding those who read newspapers frequently and those who often watch television news evaluate the Supreme Court, the branch of the national government that receives by far the smallest share of national news coverage. The results show the familiar overall pattern: People who watched the television news every day were far more likely than those who never watched to give the Supreme Court high marks. Twenty-five percent of those who watched the news every day gave the Court a rating above 80, a score awarded by only 13 percent of those who did not watch network television news. The difference may be less pronounced among newspaper readers, but the pattern was the same: Twenty-four percent of those who read the paper every day gave the Court a rating above 80, while 17 percent of those who did not read a newspaper gave the court that high of a score. Very few members of any media use group for either media source gave the Court a very negative evaluation (only 2 or 3 percent of each group gave the Court a rating of 20 or below). Even so, the overall patterns of more favorable evaluations of the Court by those who consumed more media were statistically significant for both newspaper readers and network news watchers.

This finding of high levels of support for the Court may at first seem strange, given the relative lack of attention paid to the Court by the news media, particularly television (Graber 2002). What could be happening here, though, is that people might be filling in blanks about their information and knowledge involving the Supreme Court with their overall evaluations of the political system (cf., Caldeira and Gibson 1992; Gibson and Caldeira 1992). People with high levels of media use tended to view the political system very positively, and, absent evidence to the contrary, why would they view the Court negatively? People with low levels of media use tended to view the political system less positively (but still not all that negatively). Why, then, would they be more positive about the Court?

Nevertheless, media use differences in evaluation of the judicial branch does not occur in all comparisons, or in all years. Television-dominant news consumers, print-dominant news consumers and those who used both media formats equally had very similar patterns regarding their

Table 4.5
Media Use and Evaluations of the Supreme Court

Television 2000	0 Days	1-3 Days	4-6 Days	7 Days	CHI-SQUARE (signif)
81-100 HIGH	13%	22%	17%	25%	
61-80	33%	34%	36%	32%	
41-60 NEUTRAL	46%	35%	38%	35%	.01
21-40	6%	7%	8%	6%	
0-20 LOW	3%	2%	2%	2%	

Newspaper 2000	0 Days	1-3 Days	4-6 Days	7 Days	CHI-SQUARE (signif)
81-100 HIGH	17%	17%	19%	24%	
61-80	32%	38%	36%	30%	
41-60 NEUTRAL	41%	38%	38%	37%	.03
21-40	8%	5%	4%	8%	
0-20 LOW	3%	3%	3%	2%	

Note: Percentages may not add to 100% because of rounding.

2000 assessments of the Supreme Court, far from any acceptable levels of statistical significance. A similar test of the Supreme Court using a 1992 survey (Hibbing and Theiss-Morse 1995) found no statistically significant differences among the various types of media consumers (Farnsworth 1997). Again, more frequent consumers of the news media had more positive opinions of this branch of government, or the differences between the media use groups failed to achieve statistical significance.

Summing Up (So Far)

Thus far in the chapter we have learned one thing about the patterns of media use and political support: The case against the mass media, the allegedly sinister triggers of citizen alienation and citizen negativity, has been weighed in the balance and found wanting. Test after test shows that the greater one's use of the mass media, the more positive one's views of the government and its component parts are. Every statistically significant difference found here and presented so far in this chapter points in the direction of the media building political support. Some of the other findings were inconclusive, which, of course, fails to support the charge that the news media are undermining the political system. There has not been a single instance so far of a statistically significant finding that more frequent users of the mass media are disposed more negatively toward government or its component parts than those citizens who do not make much use of newspapers and network television news. If television is as destructive to political support as many have claimed, the evidence should be in the negative—not the positive—direction.

But an additional round of testing may be in order. Perhaps it is premature at this point to credit or blame media outlets for these response patterns. Other factors may be at work, factors beyond the two variables included in the cross-tab analysis above (cf., Norris 2000). One can imagine, for example, that people choose to become television-dominant consumers of news for reasons that exist entirely separate from television: Television-dominant news consumers may be busier, less interested in reading or less literate than other news consumers, for example. None of these conditions, one might add, would tend to move a person toward focused evaluations of government and away from the more generalized perspectives. People may come to television with a mindset that seeks out generalized and somewhat simplified visions of the world, and the networks simply may be filling the need for such simplification rather than creating the desire for this approach to news. The media may still be the sources of problems, but these problems do not appear in an analysis that looks at only two variables at a time.

Political Support and Media Use: Analyses Using Several Variables

This next section exists mainly to report the additional evidence that refutes the charge that the news media undermine political support. The effects presented so far in this chapter fall into two categories: (1) People with more frequent levels of media use are more supportive of the political system and its component parts than those who use media less frequently and (2) when the results are not positive, there are no substantial differences in the opinions of people who consume very different frequency levels of mass media. The additional tests involve OLS regression equations like those used in chapters 2 and 3. These two media variables—the number of days a week a person watches the network news and the number of days a week the person reads a newspaper— are added to the variables used in those previous multivariate analyses (including those by-now-familiar measures of partisanship, ideology, education, political system trust, interpersonal trust, political efficacy and so on).

Because the media variables were insignificant in the multivariate equations in every case, a summary of the tests undertaken will suffice. Six separate OLS regressions were undertaken with exactly the same variables used in the 2000 analyses in earlier chapters. The six dependent variables tested in the six separate analyses were the questions on fair elections and on one's level of democratic satisfaction, as well as the thermometer readings for the federal government, for Bill Clinton, for the Congress and for the Supreme Court. These six separate analyses offered twelve opportunities for the two media variables to play statistically significant roles in one's levels of political support (six tests for the importance of the amount of newspaper use and six for the importance of the amount of television use). In all twelve cases, the variables failed to achieve statistical significance. When the effects of all the other variables are taken into account, any of the media use differences seen in the bivariate analyses earlier in the chapter simply disappear. The bottom line, though, remains the same: The evidence here shows repeatedly that the news media do not have as significant and sinister an effect on the American polity as many scholars have feared. The multivariate tests using data from the 2000 ANES demonstrated that the media do not undermine political support, either for the political system overall nor for any of its component parts.

CONCLUSION

Mark Twain once said, "reports of my death have been greatly exaggerated." Similarly, the reports of the damage caused to the U.S. political system by the negativity found on television news programs have been overstated greatly. The same holds for the print press, often also attacked by politicians and others for creating greater public cynicism about government in general and for creating greater hostility to individual officeholders. These findings suggest that media use is not weakening the legitimacy of the American political system. Clearly this common indictment of television, is inappropriate. Again, the same goes for the print press, which also has failed to live up to its advance billing as the trigger for considerable citizen cynicism regarding government.

The absence of findings for media effects relating to public opinion may be the legacy of the powerful political socialization trends discussed in earlier chapters. One's overall orientation regarding the political system may be developed in youth, long before one becomes a regular viewer of television news or a regular reader of a newspaper. Or, these orientations may be established more firmly in young adulthood, when few people are reading newspapers and watching the network news (see Table 4.1). Or this may be a matter of cognition. Research has shown that people are more inclined to remember—and to consider most salient—information that fits in well with one's own previous political beliefs (cf., Graber 1988; 2002). Although political socialization has been in decline among public opinion scholars in recent years, the findings in this project demonstrate clearly that further research along these lines is warranted.

The fact that television and newspapers are not the great delegitimators of government that some have thought does not, however, excuse the news media for their poor performances. A wide range of research has demonstrated that network television news in particular has been notable mainly for its triviality, its focus on strategy and personality rather than matters of substance (Farnsworth and Lichter 2003; Kerbel 1995, 1998; Patterson 1993; Sabato 1993). Perhaps if television were more substantive, the content of its newscasts would be more relevant to public views regarding the political system overall, as well as its component parts. Or perhaps not. Newspapers, after all, often do a better job than television in providing matters of substance, though even they have been marked by declining quality on a number of measures in recent decades (Farnsworth and Lichter 2003; Patterson 1993). But attention to the content of newspapers likewise failed to be a statistically significant predictor of one's political support.

There is a substantial, well-established collection of evidence that demonstrates the effectiveness of the news media's role in setting the political agenda and in framing the terms of the debate. The results here suggest, as some previous scholars have argued, that the news media encourage a focus on narrowly defined political topics: the horse race of campaigns rather than issues, the strategy of lawmaking rather than the substance of competing policy plans and the misconduct of individual political actors rather than any possible indictment of the overall political system (cf., Bennett 2001; Farnsworth and Lichter 2003; Iyengar 1991; Iyengar and Kinder 1987). Were television to address larger issues in more fundamental ways, perhaps this media content would be more relevant to public support of government in the United States.

Perhaps the real effects of media content on political support are yet to come: through the more interactive medium of the Internet (Davis 1999; Drudge 2000; Sunstein 2001). As increasing numbers of people use cyberspace as a major source of news and information in the years ahead, the negligible influence of television and newspapers seen in this chapter may be superseded by effects triggered by the information contained in this more participatory, more interactive media format. Only time will tell whether this will be the case.

These last several chapters have provided a wealth of quantitative information about the nature of public orientations toward the national government and toward the component parts of that government. So far, we have relied solely on mass survey research to investigate the public's discontent and contentment with government and politics in the United States. But these data and analyses of public opinion have told us only part of the story of political support, the quantitative approach to these questions.

In chapter 5, we will take a walk on the qualitative side. The next chapter takes a different approach to examining political support, through the use of in-depth interviews that delve behind the limited options of responses in the mass survey format. In interviews people can discuss how they feel about government in some detail, and researchers can question these citizens to make clear ambiguous statements or to settle contradictions. The interviews allow a researcher to learn a lot more about an individual's feelings than is provided by the simple formats used in mass survey research (e.g., whether one strongly agrees, agrees, is neutral, disagrees, or disagrees strongly with a given statement). While findings from interviews do not provide the level of statistical rigor found in quantitative analysis, they may provide additional information that can help enrich our understandings of public attachments to government. This supplemental approach may help provide new directions to the quantitative dimension of the study of political support.

5

"Voices in the Wilderness?": Ordinary Citizens and Political Support

The preceding chapters have examined how citizens orient themselves toward the U.S. political system as a whole and toward the component parts of that political system. But this chapter aims to deal with two important issues that remain unresolved: (1) How does interpersonal trust relate to building and/or maintaining political support? and (2) Does the citizen frustration found in mass opinion surveys trigger some interest in or support for an alternative political structure, namely, that of greater power for state governments?

In chapter 2 and chapter 3 we found little evidence that interpersonal trust is a consistently important determinant of how people feel about their government and the parts of the government. But the survey questions themselves, or at least the ones available in both the 1996 and 2000 ANES, may not be doing all that good of a job of tapping into this dimension of citizen orientation. Similarly, public opinion surveys in the United States rarely offer citizens much of an opportunity to discuss any possible alternative sovereignty, even though the presence of such a vision may be significant for a political system that generates extensive citizen frustration (Sniderman 1981).

An individual's attachment to politics can be a very complicated and a very personal thing, and such nuanced views may not be captured by the format of forced responses used in mass survey research. As a result, some researchers looking into citizen frustration with government have found it useful to supplement their research with citizen interviews (cf., Craig 1993; Tolchin 1999). This chapter turns to interviews to address these two questions, but one must recognize at the outset that this approach has its limitations. The discussions recounted in this chapter are not a representative sample: There are too few people included here to be statistically valid in any scientific sense. Further, the fact that all of that those interviewed have several things in common raises the potential that the findings can be misleading if one were to extrapolate broader trends in public opinion from this group. Nevertheless, listening to these citizens may help give us new insights into the relationship of interpersonal trust to political support and into the possibility of an alternative sovereignty in the minds of frustrated Americans. Such tentative conclusions, of course, would need to be tested in subsequent national surveys. But, at a minimum, this approach represents an important part of this project's efforts to restart the stalled paradigm of political support (cf., Farnsworth 1999a, 1999b, 2001a). The interviews also allow us to begin to address important issues that have eluded us so far in this project.

THE INTERVIEWS

This chapter will present the results of twenty face-to-face interviews conducted in Fredericksburg, Virginia, a moderately sized city located about 60 miles south of Washington, D.C., and about 60 miles north of Richmond, Virginia. To minimize the impact of ongoing developments during the interview period, all discussions occurred during the same month, June 1997.

The subjects were volunteers who responded to an advertisement published in the Saturday, May 31, 1997, and Monday, June 2, 1997, editions of the Fredericksburg, Virginia, *Free Lance–Star*. The following notice appeared in the "Help Wanted" section of the classified advertisements.

> VIRGINIA-BORN area residents over 18 being sought for research project at MWC. No expertise required. $10 for one hour interview and completed survey. Call [xxx-xxxx] for more information.

Individuals who called were told in the vaguest possible terms that the survey and interview focused on citizen feelings about government and politics. They were told that this study was not a test of knowledge but that it merely involved expressing one's own opinions. They also were told that this was not a project just for political junkies and that they should feel comfortable participating whether or not they paid much attention to politics and whether or not they voted. They were told it would be about the easiest $10 they ever would make.

Of twenty-nine telephone inquiries, a total of 25 people said they would take the survey and be interviewed. Of those 25 who agreed to participate, 20 actually kept their original or follow-up appointments. Those who did not keep their original appointments received at least two follow-up phone calls asking them to call and to reschedule for another time. Most of the interviews were about forty-five minutes in length, though a few lasted an hour.

The somewhat aggressive efforts to try to convince people to participate was a deliberate attempt to provide a diverse collection of respondents, not just those who were very interested in politics and government and felt very comfortable discussing such matters. Self-selection can be a serious problem in an interview project of this nature, but the vague newspaper advertisement and the efforts to secure the participation of everyone who called provided an interview group that consisted of more than just political junkies. Among those interviewed for this project, 25 percent said they did not vote in the 1996 presidential election, and 35 percent said "no" or "maybe" when asked if they planned to vote in Virginia's November 1997 gubernatorial election. This was a sample that did not consist solely of "political junkies," people with high levels of interest in politics.

This sample is clearly not a representative slice of the American electorate. All live within thirty miles of Fredericksburg, and all were reading the local newspaper's classified advertisements to learn about employment opportunities. What they also had in common was that they were interested in earning an extra $10. The sample was disproportionately young (65 percent under 30 years of age), disproportionately female (75 percent), disproportionately born-again Christian (30 percent) and disproportionately African American (25 percent). Yet these oversamplings are actually an advantage for this project: Younger citizens can offer special insights into future trends, and research in the earlier chapters of this work suggested that African Americans tended to be more frustrated with government on some dimensions and therefore should be considered more extensively anyway. Born-again Christians have rapidly become a key component of the Republican Party, especially in Virginia (Rozell and Wilcox 1996).

Volunteers were given a brief survey after being told that they would be identified with a first name not their own in reports on this project. The survey, which includes some of the traditional civic continuum measures as well as an extended battery asking about state government and interpersonal trust, is found in Appendix C. Background information on each of the respondents is found in Appendix D. In this report, the interviewees have been given a first name in the alphabetical order in which they participated: The first person interviewed is identified here as Anne, the second as Bonnie and so on. Males were given male names, and females were given female names. The first person, Anne, was interviewed on June 4, 1997; the twentieth and last person in the study, Theresa, was interviewed on June 25, 1997.

While several of those interviewed were college students, only one of them was a student at Mary Washington College, where the author teaches. The student had never met the interviewer, however, nor could she recall hearing him discussed in conversations with other students.

While the advertisement asked only for Virginia-born residents, two of those interviewed actually were born outside the state but moved to Virginia in the first two years of their lives. The two—identified in this project as Martha and Sarah—were retained in this study because of their close connections to the state. Both were children of Virginia parents, and both were educated throughout elementary and secondary school in Virginia. In addition, both have lived in the state as children, adolescents and adults.

The political context in June 1997 gave some reason for concern about how current events might skew responses. First, during this interview period, antigovernment terrorist Timothy McVeigh was convicted and sentenced for the Oklahoma City bombing, a topic that could have reduced citizen willingness to speak honestly against the federal government for fear of sounding like McVeigh. Perhaps because the trial was not televised, McVeigh did not appear to be relevant to these discussions in the minds of those being interviewed—no government critics brought up McVeigh's name, even to say that they were not like him.

A second major news story—though a local issue—also triggered some concern that the survey and interviews may be skewed by short-term conditions. Two young girls in the Fredericksburg area were abducted, assaulted and murdered in May 1997, shortly before the interviews. These killings triggered a reinvestigation of the 1996 murder of another area teenager in similar circumstances, and the suspect jailed on the first crime was exonerated. (These cases would remain unresolved for more than five years [Glod 2002]). Parental fears of an unidentified killer still at large, coupled with law enforcement errors in the case, could have created a climate of hostility against local governments, but that did not appear in these interviews. When these murders came up in conversation, they usually were discussed in the context of personal safety, not government and politics.

A third short-term factor was the November 1997 Virginia gubernatorial election. Lt. Gov. Donald S. Beyer Jr., the Democratic nominee, and Att. Gen. James S. Gilmore III, the Republican choice (and the eventual victor), both were unopposed in their political parties, and both began running television advertisements for the general election campaign around the interview period. But that far-off election did not seem likely to skew responses.

The small number of citizens interviewed and the things they have in common (including newspaper readership) advise strongly against overgeneralization of the findings from these twenty interviews. After all, one certainly cannot speak about the views of Virginians generally from these interviews, an admittedly small and skewed sample. This part of the project is just the starting point for further consideration of the two key issues considered in this chapter: interpersonal trust and visions of an alternative political order.

People who scour the want ads and are willing to be interviewed for an extra $10 are not the sort of individuals whose voices echo the loudest in our political system, or in much past political science research, for that matter. Political scientist Robert Lane (1962) showed the extraordinary insight that can be gained from looking into the beliefs of a small number of ordinary working-class men. The views of people on the periphery of our political system seem particularly important for a study that focuses on political support. After all, these interviewees may be more frustrated than the more well-informed and well-connected political elites who are more familiar to political scientists and who sometimes make appearances in projects in this area (Craig 1993; Tolchin 1999). The philosophy behind adding these interviews to this project is not to undermine the quantitative work of the earlier chapters, but, rather, to amplify some of the earlier findings and perhaps suggest new areas for quantitative inquiry.

The comments below are verbatim responses from the individuals interviewed. Lapses of grammar, mild profanity and examples of self-contradiction can be found in the following pages. The point here, however, is not to embarrass those people making the comments, but to illustrate as honestly and as completely as possible each person's thinking about the issues raised in this project. Indeed, the process of thinking presented in these pages suggests that public opinion is relatively informed, and the process of citizen evaluation is relatively nuanced and sophisticated.

INTERPERSONAL TRUST AND POLITICAL TRUST

Surveys consistently have shown that many people feel government officials are not very trustworthy. The same is true for the people interviewed here. What these findings show that is more novel is that oftentimes how one feels about the trustworthiness of one's fellow citizens as a whole has little to do with how one feels about the trustworthiness of government officials.

Daniel, a 32-year-old white who doesn't have much interest in politics, is a typical example. Daniel, who didn't vote in 1996 and didn't plan to vote in the November 1997 governor's race, said people were generally good. He added, though, that that assessment doesn't apply to politicians, who can and do take advantage of all kinds of special rules for their own gain.

DANIEL: There are all kinds out there, but for the most part, though, [people] are fair.

Q: How do your feelings about human nature affect your views about politicians?

DANIEL: I think they use the government to get over on anything they can. I think they are highly paid and they are not watched by the average person and anyone who is not watched or who doesn't punch a time clock—I can't say that, I don't punch a time clock [laughs]. They are paid no matter what. I don't get paid unless I get a job done, unless they have something that they see. I just don't think—what do you call it?—I forget, what kind of immunity do they have?

Q: Legislative immunity?

DANIEL: Yeah. They can do different things that everyone else can't do and it kind of goes to their head. It is like, "Let's see how much I can push and get away with."

The views regarding human nature held by Theresa, a 25-year-old white, are shaped largely by her born-again Christian beliefs. They tended toward the negative in general, and she felt government officials were even worse than ordinary people.

THERESA: We learn from the Bible that man is wicked and has an evil nature. It is only through God that we can change that. I think it all boils down to that. Today mankind as a whole is out for himself, and if you are not living for God, you are pretty much against everybody else, I think. I think that is pretty much how the country is, we are all self-centered.

Q: What about government officials, are they more trustworthy, less trustworthy or as trustworthy?

THERESA: I think they are less trustworthy. There was a line from a movie: "I'm a politician. If I am not kissing babies, I am stealing their lollipops." That is how I think of politicians—double-sided, they want to please everybody, and so, if they are trying to please everybody, they are not really trying to please you. They are just putting on an act.

Christopher, aged 24, has never voted because he said he hasn't found a politician he could trust. Besides being among the most alienated from government and most negatively disposed toward government officials, he also had a very cynical view of human nature, a low level of interpersonal trust.

CHRISTOPHER: It's just like when you read through the classified ads, you're looking for a car, let's say. You go look at a car, you're someone in my position who knows a good bit about cars, you can see it is not worth the money they are asking, and they will say, "Oh, it's good," "It's a real good vehicle" or whatever the case may be. They are going to rob you. They think they are going to get you, but they are not if you are smart enough to stay away. If you don't have that sixth sense to think about what you are doing, when you see something, if you want it bad enough, they are going to rob you, or they won't. The best people I deal with are my friends. I don't like to deal with strangers; if I do, I take it with a grain of salt. There are precautions, "Buyer Beware," because that is what happens every day in this world. Every day, every minute of the day, somebody somewhere is getting ripped off on something, and a lot of people don't understand.

Elgin, a 42-year-old African American, believes that strong laws are needed to keep political elites in check. As he discussed the issue, though, he began to change his mind and ended up more negatively disposed toward people in general than he was at the start of his comments.

ELGIN: When I say that I don't mean the average Joe Blow, I mean the ones who could, should I say . . . politicians, corporations and also people in general, too. I think we have lost something. When I grew up, your parents taught you some kind of morality. You knew that if you did something wrong you were going to get your ass whipped by the individual who caught you doing something wrong, and you were going to get your ass whipped once you got home again, too. Kids now, they don't have that same type of upbringing.

Some people, like Francine, thought of human nature inside and outside of politics in roughly the same fashion. But, because of their authority, government workers can cause more trouble for the rest of Americans, she said.

FRANCINE: The opportunity for them to do something and get away with it, and no one will know—that kind of thing just arises more when you have power. So I think it is pretty much the same type of people in the world are in government, but it is just that they have more opportunities to take advantage.

Quentin also tended to think of the people inside and outside of government as made of roughly the same moral fiber and not very deserving of trust. But he said he particularly was concerned by how frequently even decent people seem to be corrupted by Washington.

> QUENTIN: It is hard to trust people, it is hard to give people breaks, and they take advantage—you give a person a foot and they take a yard. Everyone is in it for themselves, and it is just so hard to trust people. . . .
>
> [later, on politicians] I don't believe it is them themselves. I think it is the system. The system leads to corruption, it turns honest—maybe not totally honest, I don't think anyone is totally honest all the time. . . . Take someone who wants to go to Washington to do a good job and in his campaigns is saying he is going to reform and he really and truly believes that, and when he or she gets there, the system is going to corrupt that person a lot. Maybe some of them are more corrupt, but on the whole I don't think they are.
>
> Q: So what should we do?
>
> QUENTIN: The system has to be changed . . . the special interests, the money. How it would be changed, I don't know. I wish I knew, but the system has to be overhauled, something has to be done.

Part of the reason for these differing types of linkages between political trust and personal trust may be because people have very complex views of trust. These interviews in particular show two very different kinds of interpersonal trust—the level one would trust people generally and the level one would trust people one has met at least face-to-face. There seems to be a sort of community trust, or a trust of one's neighbors, that is quite different from interpersonal trust. Interpersonal trust, as it generally is conceived, relates to one's general views concerning human nature, but these interviews suggest that the interpersonal trust relating to strangers can be quite different from that relating to acquaintances in the neighborhood. Roberta was one of four people (20 percent) in the survey who said they disagreed strongly with the statement that people were basically fair. But, she said she would let all five of her neighbors borrow her television for an evening, even though she doesn't really know them.

> ROBERTA: People have gotten to the point you can't trust anyone. You really can't trust anybody anymore. I don't know what it is. They don't have any respect for another human being anymore. It is all just fading away. It is like just every man for himself. That is how I see it. I don't think people were raised to be that way, but I think that, with things the way they are in the world, it has made them that way. It is not the way they want to be, it is the way they have to be to live

day to day and to survive. I do believe that. That is a sad way to be, but that is the way it is now. It is all about survival.

Q: I asked you a question about television—

ROBERTA: Oh, the TV, borrowing it. Well, my neighborhood, I would loan it to them and I would think I would get it back. Because where I live are elderly people on either side, and then on down there are two young couples with small children—you know, hardworking people. So I think I would trust them, I would. You have to give a person a chance, first of all, you have to give a person a chance. If then they give you a reason to distrust them, then you have to do what you have to do. But I would trust them with a TV, I would. And now, mind you, these are people that I've never been inside their homes. I speak to them when I see them outside; you know, everybody speaks, everybody is friendly. But if they asked, I think I would actually loan it to them. And that is saying a lot, coming from me the way I am. I'm surprised I answered it that way, but I would loan it to them. I would.

Sarah is another person who wants to trust people. Sarah and Roberta are two of the eight people (40 percent) who said they would loan their televisions for an evening to all of their neighbors living in the five houses or apartments closest to them. Another four people (20 percent) said they would trust four of the five neighbors, while two people (10 percent) said they would trust three of the five and three people (15 percent) said they would trust two of the five. Only one (Christopher) said none of his neighbors could be trusted with a television, and two other people (Irene and Nancy) said only one neighbor could be trusted. Sarah, who is of the most trusting group, said she had taken chances on people she probably wouldn't take if she had stopped to think about it.

SARAH: I'm probably more trusting than I should be. I am a very positive person towards people. I try to like them. If I am proved wrong, that is part of life. But I'm not looking at a person and saying, "I'm not going to trust you."

Q: I notice you are willing to trust all your neighbors with your television.

SARAH: Well, the television couldn't be taken out anyway because it is hooked up to cable. Yes, but I have my friends, and if they wanted to borrow my television, sure, I would loan it to them. I've loaned my car to a complete stranger, which I thought was very foolish to do. She was the paper carrier and her car broke down. She had a couple of children and she had to finish her route, and I gave her my car. I thought, "You are really dumb." I did it, but I don't think I would do it again. But it is my trusting nature.

This study developed this television-loaning question to measure a distinct kind of interpersonal trust—a willingness to take a risk for one's neighbor. Nearly everyone has a television, a relatively valuable and somewhat fragile possession, and everyone has neighbors. Determining which of one's neighbors one would trust and which ones one would not trust forced people to consider interpersonal trust carefully. The comments on this question, including those not recounted in this chapter, consistently indicate that a very different kind of evaluation went on here than in one's basic evaluation of human nature.

This is an area where one should proceed with caution. Citizens of this relatively small southern city, particularly those who are native to this state, clearly do not represent America as a whole. The population of the Fredericksburg metropolitan area at the time of these interviews was roughly 200,000. Area residents generally are clustered in small neighborhoods and subdivisions that dot the relatively small city (which contains roughly 25,000 citizens) and the surrounding counties. The area is not all that urban—indeed, aside from one relatively new high-rise, the downtown skyline looks about the same as it did in photographs taken a century ago. Community trust, therefore, may be much stronger here than in many other urban places. But, while the percentages may be different in other places, that does not necessarily undermine the importance of community trust for democratic satisfaction. The decline of community trust may be something that has occurred in some places along with urbanization and suburbanization (cf., Greider 1992).

The results here offer a possible explanation for why the ANES measures of interpersonal trust generally did not seem to play important roles in predicting one's level of political support throughout this project. One would have expected, given the conclusions of Robert Putnam (1995a, 1995b, 2000), that such measures would be an important part of explaining one's level of satisfaction with the political world. Both of the ANES questions relate to basic issues of human nature, but that may not be the most important—or, perhaps, the most direct—measure of personal trust. How one feels about one's neighbors may be even more important for understanding a person's level of interpersonal trust. As communitarians have suggested, expanding and strengthening a civic community fosters a healthy polity, one in which interpersonal trust can thrive (cf., Boyte 1990, 1994).

Taken as a whole, these observations suggest that Putnam's thesis has not been given a full test in the quantitative section of this project and that only speculations based on qualitative findings are possible at this point. If questions analogous to that of the television loaning make their way into national surveys, one might want to consider the ways that "community trust," one's willingness to trust one's neighbors, can help build the more general "interpersonal trust" that relates to one's overall views concerning human nature. Even with the limited sample here, we still have some indication that this community trust might have a lot a more to do with democratic satisfaction than does interpersonal trust. But this is, of course, a very tentative finding given the small and distinct sample used here. If we someday find a stronger relationship for community trust and democratic satisfaction in a national study, that would be powerful evidence in support of the idea that "bowling alone" does indeed have the troublesome consequences suggested by past research.

THE COMMONWEALTH OF VIRGINIA: AN ALTERNATIVE SOVEREIGN?

Because the American political system has remained intact since the eighteenth century, many political scientists have argued that any substantial structural change is highly unlikely, even in the face of extensive citizen discontent (Huntington 1981; Sniderman 1981). Political scientists have long argued that a citizen's feelings toward the institutions of government are very slow to change in the face of short-term disappointments (cf., Easton and Dennis 1969). Indeed, questions of any such alternative sovereignty rarely have been considered since political scientist Paul Sniderman (1981) found so little evidence of any alternative plan in the 1970s for rebuilding our political order. The Fredericksburg area interviews offer a preliminary reconsideration of this vital, but not often tested, assumption.

The Virginia Context

Of all the American states, Virginia can lay claim to the most thorough control by an oligarchy. Political power has been closely held by a small group of leaders who, themselves and their predecessors, have subverted democratic institutions and deprived most Virginians of a stake in government. . . . [Virginia] is a political museum piece. . . . (Key 1949:19)

In the half century since these words were published much has changed in the world. But some things remain the same in Virginia. While the political machine of Senator Harry Byrd itself has faded and many of its outmoded philosophies, such as "massive resistance" to desegregation and "Pay as You Go" capital improvements, have been discarded, many of the machine's values still permeate today's Virginia. The state (while Virginia is technically a commonwealth, the two terms will be used interchangeably here) as a whole remains generally conservative, still tends to be dominated by political elites and remains relatively hostile to national government encroachment on what Virginia's elected officials envision to be areas of state authority (Atkinson 1992; Fickett 1985; Wilkinson 1968).

Yet it is not fair to shade Virginia in the monochromatic color of reaction. Virginia, though clearly one of the country's more conservative states, was the first (and, as of this writing, remains the only) state to have elected an African American governor. The enfranchised African American electorate, together with the growing numbers of transplanted (and often ideologically moderate) citizens from northern states, do battle in this commonwealth with the remnants of the conservative Byrd machine (many members of which are now Republicans) and with a revived Christian Right led by Rev. Jerry Falwell and Rev. Pat Robertson, both of whom make Virginia their home (Edds 1990; Fickett 1985; Rozell and Wilcox 1996).

The issue of state government power versus national government power remains a key issue in modern Virginia politics, well after the years of massive resistance to desegregation and the dominance of the Byrd machine (Atkinson 1992; Edds 1990). But one should not overstate the distinctiveness of Virginia on this issue. The call of states' rights resonate strongly in many parts of the country besides Virginia, including other areas of the South and some western states where citizens and governments are concerned about extensive federal landholdings (Gugliotta 1995; Wood 1995). Greater state and local control also has been a part of the Republican Party agenda under former U.S. House Speaker Newt Gingrich (1995) and the platforms of recent Republican presidential candidates, including U.S. Senator Bob Dole (R-Kan.) and President George W. Bush.

Average citizens can distinguish clearly among the various levels of government, according to national survey research. Table 5.1 shows the results of ANES questions that asked people the level of government in which they have the most and least confidence.

In 1996, the federal government was overwhelmingly the choice as the source of the least faith and confidence: forty-eight percent said they were troubled most by government at the national level, as compared to 34 percent selecting the local level and only 19 percent picking the state level. When asked about the most confidence, the pattern was reversed: The states finished first with 37 percent giving them the highest mark, as compared to the 33 percent who most favored local government and the 30 percent who preferred the national government. (These two questions were not asked in the 2000 ANES). Clearly, the idea of taking some power away from Washington and giving it to state governments finds a ready nationwide audience of citizens.

Table 5.1
Evaluations of Levels of Government: ANES Measures

LEVEL MOST

The percentage saying they have the most faith and confidence in this level of government.

	1996	1976	1974	1972	1968
FEDERAL	30%	32%	32%	46%	50%
STATE	37%	28%	30%	24%	20%
LOCAL	33%	40%	38%	30%	30%

LEVEL LEAST

The percentage saying they have the least faith and confidence in this level of government.

	1996	1976	1974	1972	1968
FEDERAL	48%	47%	47%	27%	32%
STATE	19%	20%	16%	25%	24%
LOCAL	34%	33%	37%	48%	45%

Note: Percentages may not all add up to 100% because of rounding.

In fact, the respondents to these ANES questions were more strongly in favor of increased state power than were the Fredericksburg area interviewees to similar questions. Of those interviewed for this project, 45 percent said they had the least faith in the federal government, 30 percent said the state, 15 percent said local government, one person said "none" and another did not know. The federal government was also the source of the most faith or confidence for 30 percent, while 20 percent favored state government 15 percent favored the local government, and 25 percent said "none." One person said "all," and another (Nancy) said she did not know.

The interview group was much more polarized than the national survey. People had strong feelings both for and against the national government in the "faith and confidence" questions, while the pattern for the national questions showed a parallel response pattern across the two measures. Here one may speculate that the interview results are in part a legacy of the Byrd political machine's overwhelming dominance of Virginia politics during this past century. The machine's extraordinarily strong hostility toward national power may have created two state cultures existing simultaneously: one of acolytes very loyal to the state and one of enemies who may see Washington as the only possible counter to the power wielded within Virginia by the Byrd machine and its partisans. For much of the twentieth century, citizens in this state were not defined by whether they were Democrats or Republicans, but by whether they were pro-Byrd or anti-Byrd (Black 1983; Dabney 1971; Fickett 1985; Key 1949; Wilkinson 1968). The state clearly has shown itself to be a curious political jurisdiction in electoral politics: Virginia is the only state in the country to have ever elected an African American governor (Douglas Wilder in 1989), and a few years later it came quite close to sending Ollie North, a conservative talk show host and key Iran-Contra figure, to the U.S. Senate in 1994 (Edds 1990; Rozell and Wilcox 1996). The interview questions and electoral results may be evidence of a schizophrenic state political culture.

These two questions also may be unstable from individual to individual because of the complicated nature of this question: Faith and confidence relate to the two very different evaluations. One part of the question may elicit an emotional reaction, the other a more performance-based calculation. In addition, the interviewees were given the chance to choose "all" or "none" to both of these questions, an option not offered in the national survey. This also could skew the interviewee response patterns when compared to the ANES survey.

Further consideration of other questions in the survey also raises concerns about how much attention we should pay to responses to the faith and confidence questions. Two related questions asked of the interviewees were concerned with the level of "love" one has for the United States and for Virginia; responses showed that enthusiasm for Virginia (in the interview group, at least) may be greater than the faith and confidence questions suggest. Of the six interviewees who said they had the least confidence in the state government, four nevertheless said they had an "extremely strong" or a "very strong" love of Virginia. Of the six who said they had the most confidence in the national government, four said they had as much love for Virginia as for the United States. These two "love" questions were not asked in the 1996 ANES, so no comparison can be made to the national sample in this regard.

We therefore are left with two discrepancies. The first is between a consistent national sample and an inconsistent sample of interviewees on the faith and confidence questions. The second involves only the interviewees and their differing responses to the faith and confidence questions and the love questions. These conflicting patterns demonstrate the need for probing through interviews to determine what people were thinking when they answered these questions. The comments tend to be polarized somewhat less than some of the original limited responses to the survey questions. Upon further reflection, many of those comparing the state government and the national government said they were frustrated particularly with the national government. The pro-state nature of many comments may be a result of knowing more about what the national government does and hearing more about the problems in Washington than the problems in Richmond. The comments in the next section demonstrate that there is a great love of and support for Virginia among many of those interviewed, a finding more consistent with the love questions than the faith and confidence questions. These comments also show that there is a base of citizen discontent in Virginia, particularly among African Americans and some women. While an overall diagnosis of schizophrenia may be a bit premature based on the evidence available here, what we do have suggests that further investigation along these lines should be part of a subsequent research agenda.

States may be popular in this country (and with many of the interviewees) primarily because they do not have the unilateral authority to do all that much and therefore are insulated from much criticism about governmental performance. Even so, public opinion concerning state power represents an important new area of inquiry for the study of political support, one that has triggered some theoretical musings from a few researchers but not much study involving mass public opinion. State power, therefore, also seems an important area to consider given the relatively high marks that citizens nationally have tended to give state governments.

Some political scientists also have looked at greater power for state government as a means of dealing with high levels of citizen frustration with the more distant national government. Increasing the power of state governments is a natural path for a federal government to follow when it is under fire for taking on too many responsibilities (Bennett and Bennett 1990). Increasing the power of state government in some areas also may make sense on the grounds of efficiency (Herbers 1987; Rivlin 1992). States may be able to tailor their policies more precisely to meet distinct needs within their borders, for example, leading to a more efficient allocation of resources than is the one-size-fits-all national model.

As much as citizens may be frustrated with the national government, reducing the totality of government functions is not an attractive option, either for the citizens or their elected leaders, according to past research (Bennett and Bennett 1990).

> Americans are no longer struggling with a choice. They have made a choice and it is for big government. The degree to which they are comfortable with the centralization of government may vary at times. But when that concern does arise, government does not withdraw from providing its many services and benefits; instead it shifts surface provision to another level, most recently to that of the state. (Bennett and Bennett 1990:137)

Political scientist Martha Derthick (1987) said that consideration of states' rights no longer should be saddled with the past racist connotations of the term. One should be able to consider the question of the relative efficiency of state and national governments on their merits, not on the basis of past unsavory associations from the 1950s and 1960s.

> Until now, arguments favoring the states' side in any dispute over federalism suffered fatally from the burden of the South's deviant social system. Whether or not blacks have been successfully integrated into American society (a separate question), there can be little doubt that the South as a region has been integrated. That change, even if achieved very largely by the instrumentalities of the federal government, holds the possibility that the case for the states can at last begin to be discussed on its merits. (Derthick 1987:72)

Communitarians and some other liberals likewise have supported the idea that more localized orientations may be the mechanism through which politics can serve to educate citizens more effectively (cf., Boyte 1990; Chrislip 1994; Kunde 1994). In part, this is because locally based problems are closer to home and seem both easier for citizens to understand and particularly amenable to local action.

> Rather than dry "civics courses," exhortations to vote, or protest politics, we need to show how public engagement can be a satisfying theater of action and development. Americans need to get the message: the public realm offers many pleasures and opportunities for constructive use of power beyond claiming unique possession of justice and right. The basic premise of democratic politics needs to shift from protest to citizen problem-solving. (Boyte 1990:518)

Some scholars, however, have their doubts about the effectiveness of more localized governments when compared to national authorities (Kaase and Newton 1995). While they sometimes may be more responsive, they also may be more easily corrupted (Kushma 1988). Yet, at the same time, this may make them more responsible to their often relatively more homogenous state electorates. Researchers have found, for example, a very high correlation between a state citizenry's public opinion and the policies of that state government (Erickson, Wright and McIver 1993). This pattern held for both liberal and conservative states.

Loving and Loathing the Commonwealth

The twenty people surveyed in this project were generally very proud of Virginia as a state. Eleven of those interviewed (55 percent) in the study said their love of Virginia was "extremely strong" or "very strong." Only two of the twenty interviewees gave the most negative response: "not very strong." Despite their varying backgrounds, the interviewees consistently expressed great love for the state in ways that had little to do with their feelings about the particulars of state government. The one clear cleavage—and we consider this difference throughout this the remainder of this chapter—was racial. African Americans in particular were much less enthralled with Virginia overall. But let us consider first the outpouring of love from the majority of the area residents interviewed.

They were asked to say what made them proud about Virginia and what made them not proud about the state. The initial reactions to the state often had to do with the fact that it was home, and an attractive and well-loved home at that. The fact that all of these people had lived in Virginia since birth, or virtually since birth, may have affected the nature of their responses on this point somewhat, but this aesthetic orientation toward one's love of a state is an interesting finding nevertheless.

DANIEL: I like the scenery. I like the countryside. I don't know what specifically, but I have just always liked Virginia. I have been in the military, my father was in the Navy, that is why I was born in Norfolk, Virginia. I have been around in different places and I like them, but it is just that I could never see myself moving from Virginia.

MARTHA: This is where our country grew from, where it started. There is so much culture around. I grew up being dragged from Jamestown to Yorktown, doing all the sites, and somewhere along the way learning to like that, too. I think it is very impressive, and here we are just minutes away from where it all began.

QUENTIN: I think it has so much history, so much to offer. So many great leaders of this country have come just from within this one little fifty-mile radius from here. So many great Americans have come from this state, although the state seceding from the union and slavery was here for a long time—and there is still racism here. But, generally, it is a beautiful state. I've gone from east to west, west to east and north to south; there are so many things to be proud of. We have a beautiful state capitol, beautiful colleges, a well-educated population and we are right next to all the power of D.C., so it is a perfect place to live.

THERESA: I was the first in my family to be born in Virginia and I have always been very proud of that. I enjoy being a Virginian, one of the first states and all. I'm glad my daughters were born here. It is really one of the prettier states in the country.

Q: Are there times when you are not proud of Virginia?

THERESA: Not so much as I am disappointed with the country. I can't think of specific times I am not proud of Virginia.

Q: Ever think about leaving?

THERESA: I did move away for a few months for a relationship that didn't work out. I missed it a lot. Ohio was beautiful, I loved the state, but I missed home. I was very glad to get back home.

Sometimes, as was the case with Hannah, who said her love for Virginia was somewhere between "very strong" and "somewhat strong," just not being able to think of anything negative about the state was enough to make one feel positive.

HANNAH: I guess I put that because I didn't have any strong reason why I didn't like Virginia.

Daniel, who said in the written survey that he had an "extremely strong" love for Virginia, said later in the interview that he couldn't explain why he chose that option.

DANIEL: I don't know enough about the state government to like it or dislike it.

Throughout the debates in this chapter, Christopher has been one of the most alienated interviewees. He described himself as financially on the edge and he said he didn't vote and didn't trust strangers at all. But he said he adored Virginia and described his love for the state as "very strong," the second most positive option.

CHRISTOPHER: Beautiful state, well taken care of, a lot of history— history would have to be the biggest thing, the first thing that would come into my head, especially around here. . . . All in all I would have to say Virginia is a pretty good place. . . .

[later] If I move it would probably be to another county in Virginia. I don't see myself leaving the state.

People who felt pretty positive about the state generally had few negative comments to make about Virginia, even when specifically asked, "Are there times when you are not proud of Virginia?" Odetta said she had an "extremely strong" love of state; Quentin said his love for Virginia was "very strong."

ODETTA: I can't think of any specifics. I'm sure I have disagreed with something Virginia has done, but I don't remember.

QUENTIN: Quite often, but not as often as I am of the United States. Slavery and stuff like that, scandals, like. . . . I can't think of anything else. It is a beautiful state.

The interviewing revealed a dramatic racial gap in feelings about Virginia. The two people with the least love for Virginia were both African American (Irene and Nancy), and the three other African Americans in the study (Elgin, George and Roberta) were three of the six people who gave the second most negative response about the state (the other three in that group were Bonnie, Julie and Laura). Not one of the five African Americans—who ranged in age from 21 to 42—in these interviews said they had an "extremely strong" or "very strong" love of Virginia. In contrast, eleven of the fifteen whites fell into those two most positive groups, and a twelfth wrote in the survey that her love of Virginia was between "very strong" and "somewhat strong."

Q: What comes to mind when I say "state or commonwealth of Virginia"?

ELGIN: A joke [laughs].

Q: How so?

ELGIN: Because of the fact that you have a few, a privileged few, that basically have run this state for such a long time. People in this state—I might be wrong in my assessment of this—but people don't take an interest. It is like, "Okay, as long as I can do my thing and get by." But I don't think people are as politically active as in other places, like Pennsylvania and New York. They just don't have that interest. I have to say, when I have conversations with people about current events and all the rest, they could not be concerned one way or the other, most of them.

ROBERTA: Sometimes I think this state is—I don't know, Virginia is a beautiful state, but it is strict; they are very strict. To me, their rules don't change, they don't bend. Whatever the rules are, that is the way they are, that is how they are going to stay forever. The rules are too strict. . . . I don't like the taxes much either. They tax you for everything here, I don't like that.

Q: You want to get out of Virginia?

ROBERTA: I would love to get out of Virginia. I would love to get out of Virginia. I've always said, you know, if the opportunity comes again where I could leave, I'm gone. I'll come to visit, but as far as living here, I would rather not live here.

This criticism of the state should not be an unexpected response to a state that was the capital of the Confederacy, a region that was at the center of many bloody Civil War battles (and is now filled with battle-field parks and monuments), and a state that was at the center of the struggle against school desegregation. But what may be surprising is the extent to which such strong feelings are held by the children of deseg-regation—all of the African Americans in this interview project were born after the Supreme Court's *Brown v. Board of Education, Topeka* de-cision of 1954, and the youngest was born in the mid-1970s. This may demonstrate the effects of socialization from one's family, that older ideas may be passed on from generation to generation even though the external environment has changed, at least somewhat. A distrust trig-gered by the actions of political leaders three decades ago or more still seems to haunt the state. This pattern also may suggest that less has changed for African Americans in Virginia than some people think. Elgin and Roberta both felt that the state was dominated by people too sym-pathetic to the old ways of doing things. Both had left the area for the North—Elgin lived in Pennsylvania for several years and Roberta had spent some time in New Jersey—but both felt the pull of family and, somewhat grudgingly, returned to this area.

African Americans in this project, by the way, had considerably greater love for the nation than the state. Of the five, only two (Elgin and Irene) remained in the two most negative categories, while the other three moved into the two most positive categories: George and Nancy said their love for America was "extremely strong," while Roberta said hers was "very strong." All five were in the two most negative categories when discussing their feelings about Virginia.

Of course not every critic of Virginia was African American. But when whites expressed objections to the state—which occurred much less fre-quently—it usually centered on one key issue: the state personal prop-erty tax. Virginia residents are required to pay annual taxes for their motor vehicles, and, in the case of relatively new vehicles, the state tax can run hundreds of dollars a year. Both major party candidates for governor in 1997 made plans to reduce that controversial tax key parts of their campaigns (Farnsworth 2002).

> ANNE: When I have to keep paying all this money . . . and I always keep paying and paying and paying. I didn't even get all of my money back for my taxes, and I called them and they were like, "We are spending it because you didn't pay all your personal property taxes." It is all this money that I have to keep paying, just Virginia, alone. So I am not happy I have to pay out all this money.

> ODETTA: Different tax laws I think are very unfair, especially on the state level, like re-taxing you for your car every year. You should be able to pay your tax and be done with it instead of having to pay your tax to get a county sticker.

Evaluating Richmond's Performance

The basic good feelings that most of these Virginians have toward their home state appeared to be based on hearing little criticism about the state. For this group, feelings about the national government do not appear to be of much relevance to evaluations of one's own state. When asked to say why they love Virginia, people routinely spoke of the Blue Ridge Mountains, the state's long history and other vague and emotional-laden recollections. When asked more specifically about their feelings concerning the state government, the limited extent of the information on which their evaluations of the state were based became quite clear.

> GEORGE: [Virginia] is more distant. I really don't know that much about Virginia government. You know every year they hand out some pamphlets to read about who you are going to elect, and you see a couple of commercials on TV. That is about all I get.

> LAURA: I haven't really followed Richmond politics that much. I have concentrated on what is going on in Washington, what is going on in the White House, the president.

> SARAH: I think it is a beautiful state, and as far as politics in Virginia I feel a little iffy about it. I think [Gov. Gerald L.] Baliles did a good job, I think our present governor [George Allen] is doing a good job, I think in any situation you are not going to agree 100 percent. I love Virginia.

ANNE: State [government] has always been a little hard for me to understand. National is more, I'd say, publicized, and you hear about things going on nationally more than in your state.

Q: Do you think Virginia is well run?

ANNE: Not really. It is okay, but there are, like, a lot of weird laws, and I know that we kill something like the second largest number of people on death row, besides Texas, and we are tied with Florida. I don't like that.

Roberta felt particularly torn in her evaluation of the specifics of state government. Though she rated the national government as more deserving of her affection, she felt that smaller groups of people are more likely to be more responsive than the larger national government. At the same time, she freely admitted she really didn't know much about what the state government has been doing.

ROBERTA: The government in Richmond . . . I live here in this state, and I should be ashamed to say this, but I don't pay a whole lot of attention to it. Most of the time I hear about government, it is about Washington. Like I said, they have to work with what they have to work with. I guess if I had to trust either one, if I really had to trust that one or the one in D.C., I think I would trust the one in Richmond more, because I don't think there are as many of them as those ones up in Washington. I think a small group of people can make a better decision more so than a whole bunch of people can.

Julie had a similar perspective. Again, without any clear knowledge about the workings or the responsiveness of state government, she said she just felt people in Richmond would be more responsive than those in Washington.

JULIE: Say I have some great idea—I would have no idea how to go about getting my idea to someone important in Washington. But it seems like I might be able to just drive down to Richmond, knock on some doors and ask some people where to go. It seems like I would be able to get someone to listen to me in Richmond.

Q: Have you ever been to Richmond to do that?

JULIE: No.

Q: Have you ever known anyone who has been to Richmond to do that?

JULIE: No.

This finding that affection for Virginia may stem from unfamiliarity is a pattern that researchers have often found in studies relating to media coverage of Congress. People often love their members—who usually don't get much news coverage, and what little coverage they get tends to be positive—but tend to feel negatively about Congress as a collective, which gets much more critical media coverage (Asher and Barr 1994; Cook 1989; Robinson 1981).

The lack of specific knowledge with which to evaluate the performance of state government extended in many cases even to the most visible public official: Governor George Allen, who had run the state for three and a half years at the time of these interviews. Interviewees were asked, "What do you think of Governor Allen?"

ANNE: I really don't know.

BONNIE: No real personal opinions. I haven't really focused in on him a lot. I haven't read too much about him or seen much on the news.

Kate, a 46-year-old social worker with an "extremely strong" love for Virginia, spoke of her adoration for the state's natural beauty, a thought frequently expressed above. She clearly had her doubts about Governor Allen, but notice how she came back to a generally positive evaluation of this state even in the midst of her criticism:

KATE: I don't like our current administration. I think they do some stupid things, but I don't think that reflects on Virginia. Virginia has a history that I can't say we are proud of, but we can't rewrite it. It happened. I guess the bottom line is that I can't say there has been a time when I haven't proud of the state.

Christopher seemed dramatically more satisfied with the performance of government officials in Richmond than with those in Washington, though he did say he expected more from his state government.

CHRISTOPHER: Some of the laws I think are good, they just need to work on some other things to make them better.

Q: How could they make things better?

CHRISTOPHER: I really don't know how to say they can make them better, I just know that things could be better than they are now. I know that right now there is a lot of homeless in the state of Virginia, there is a lot of people who don't have jobs and are more than able to get the jobs. The problem is they just don't have enough space to give everybody these jobs. I know myself, I've been a job-hopper my-self, and I know what it is like to hit the street every day, trying to find a place to work; you make a hard living, and you do it every day. This job that I have now, I've had it for a year and a half, and I am probably going to lose it here soon.

Again the interviews revealed a racial gap in that African Americans seemed the harshest in their evaluation of the state. The pattern that we saw with respect to love for Virginia also was found with respect to evaluating the state's performance. Elgin's earlier complaints about con-tinued rule by a "privileged few" in Virginia were echoed by Irene, who, at 21 years of age was the youngest African American interviewed for this project.

> IRENE: Just from what I see, and based on other states when it comes to laws and things like that, it seems like we are still kind of backward. I guess I was thinking we weren't in the South—that it was an in-between kind of state—but a lot of the laws are very southern and behind the times.

If she could change one thing about the state, Irene said she would improve the diversity of political elites.

> IRENE: Change the people in power, the officials. Get some more diverse and younger people in there, not the good old boys.

This racial gap in attitudes is something that really has not been con-sidered all that extensively in discussions of whether to give state gov-ernments more power. Since many of the leading advocates of devolution in politics today tend to be Republican (cf., Gingrich 1995), and since African Americans are not a part of the Republican electoral coalition, this disparity in views may not have gotten the attention it deserves. Further study of this part of the states' rights argument seems an important part of evaluating the utility and the appropriateness of this policy. These interviews, after all, can offer only a warning that African Americans may feel very disenfranchised under a system that expands the power of state governments. More extensive survey work is necessary to determine the pervasiveness of this opinion uncovered here.

What Would Enhanced Power for Virginia Mean?

Those who wanted to see Virginia have more power tended to argue that the national government has too much to handle and that Virginia's government could do a better job of tailoring policies to match the particular needs of the state.

JULIE: Virginia just has Virginia to deal with. It is smaller, it has less people. Richmond would have a better idea what to do—rather than Washington having to make laws for the whole entire country.

PAULINE: State governments are much closer. They know what you want more. It is easier to get in touch with them. They represent a smaller constituency, so they can actually listen and implement what people suggest. I think they can listen better, and they do.

LAURA: I thought that was the way the Constitution started out with. The states were supposed to run the people and the federal government was there for the common defense, for protecting us from outside forces. The state was supposed to run things. The [federal] government was supposed to create the army, the intelligence—if somebody is creating a bomb to be used against us we had better know about it and be ready for it—now the federal government is in everything. It is just incredible. . . . Richmond is local. It knows what the problems are of the state. The federal government is seeing global.

SARAH: I think the states ought to have power over their own state and the big government ought to get out of the states' business.

Q: What kinds of things should states have more control over?

SARAH: I think the abortion law, for one thing; I think that ought to be a statewide thing. And I don't know, but there are probably many others in that field. States know their own people, and the government is a big mass over the whole country, and the state ought to have more input over their people.

Note the above comments sometimes contain candid admissions on the part of the interviewees that they had the impression or the expectation that the state would be more responsive. They did not say that the state *has been* more responsive. In fact, sometimes people who explicitly criticized the performance of state government nevertheless endorsed the idea of greater state power. Martha, who objected to the state's performance on education, was still a fan of enhanced state power. Her explanation, like those above, was that the states seemed closer to the people than the national government. Like the others, she admitted that this opinion was based on a perception, not on evidence of past performance.

MARTHA: I don't think the country will necessarily benefit from a top-heavy government. States are told what they can and can not do on a daily basis by several hundred men and women in Washington even though they aren't there [in the states] and aren't seeing things on a day-to-day basis. It bothers me having the idea of having a national government to regulate for everyone in all the states what you should be doing. The states are more effective governments, and they spread out the power. Why have state governments if they aren't going to have power?

[Later] They may or may not be [more responsive]. I guess our state legislators seem to be more accessible, and that might simply just be a perception that I have.

In the same way that some critics of Virginia's performance still found themselves arguing for more power for state government, some fans of Virginia didn't necessarily want to see the state take on additional responsibilities. Theresa, who was so proud of being the first of her family to be born in Virginia, was one of those who saw problems with enhanced state power, as did Quentin, who found less to dislike about Virginia than about the United States.

THERESA: We could become divided. It would be a lot easier for the country to fall apart if states had more of their own power than the country as a whole. That could be very difficult.

QUENTIN: We shouldn't have, like, an extremely strong central government. The states should have certain powers. It's ridiculous. I mean, you can go from one state to another and have different laws enacted, and it just becomes a total mess in my opinion, especially when it comes to different laws the states will have—instead of the [federal] government handing out money for certain programs, the states will be handing out money, and who knows what they are going to do.

For some, how one felt about greater state power depended on Richmond's performance. For Bonnie, who was among the most critical white interviewees concerning Virginia, it was a question of high taxes. For Francine, who was disposed more positively toward the state, it was Governor Allen's initial unwillingness to accept federal money for education because of concerns that doing so would involve the surrender of some state autonomy to Washington.

Q: What do you think things would be like in Virginia if Virginia had more power and the federal government had less?

BONNIE: I would have to move [laughs].

Q: Why is that?

BONNIE: The cost of living is so expensive as it is here now. I always joke with my mom and say Virginia is still stuck in colonial times because they moved away from England to get away from the taxes, but yet, this is one of the highest—there are so many taxes in Virginia compared to some of the other places we have lived. It is a nice state and most people here tend to have a higher standard of living, versus, like, North Carolina.

FRANCINE: It is not that I think the federal government should have all the power, but I think right now states have too much sometimes. For example, there was just this Goals 2000 thing, I guess it was last year, and Virginia doesn't get it. It is just because Governor Allen doesn't want Virginia to get it because he doesn't want it to deduct from any of the state's power. I think it is important. I'd like to have more money for education in Virginia. The fact that the states can even make that decision to take the money away from schools makes me angry.

For Elgin, an African American, the idea of getting a national consensus on public policy issues seemed like a sensible approach, particularly given the attitudes he perceived among state officials concerning the less well-off.

ELGIN: When you give it to the states, I think that is a little scary, because of the fact that the states have their own hidden agendas about a lot of things, you know—Texas, California—and I am a little scared about that. If you have a centralized thing, then you have to get everybody's consensus. There is such a closed community in this state, that is what scares me about it.

Q: What about Virginia?

ELGIN: I'm just thinking about the time I was growing up. . . . The war was over, but some people think the South shall rise again, and that kind of scares me. Especially when it comes to minimum wage and the people who need a little help. I feel a special interest for them because they are going to be the ones hurt if they get more power. I think they are going to say, "The hell with this," "The hell with that"—community service programs and all the rest of that. So I'm kind of scared about that. There are a lot of people I think if the state had more power they would just turn their back on.

Anne, who said she had a "very strong" love of Virginia, also had a bit of doubt concerning whether the state would be as interested in taking care of the needy as the federal government has been.

ANNE: Probably there would be tighter laws, stricter. Things would be watched more closely. They might not give anyone much welfare, then. That part might not be too bad, but—I'm not sure—they might also take it away from people who need it.

CONCLUSION

The overall pattern found in this chapter was one of federal frustration and state satisfaction. According to the interviews, these feelings stem from the continuing disappointment citizens have been experiencing with respect to the national government. By explicitly positing a more powerful state government as the alternative to the Washington-dominant status quo, this section of the project examined questions of political support in a different direction than that of previous researchers, who found themselves without a base of comparison (Sniderman 1981). For nearly all of these interviewees, expanded state power was at least a debatable alternative to the Washington-dominant system that now exists.

The key reason for public disappointment with the national government was expressed in these interviews as it has been expressed before: the poor performance of Washington. Our interviewees felt that Washington needed to reduce the influence of special interests, deal more effectively with declining economic opportunities for the needy, reverse the ever-growing gap between rich and poor and, above all, give people the sense that politicians in Washington are listening to ordinary folk. That these concerns were expressed so strongly even during the economic boom of 1997 only underscores their importance to these citizens.

These citizens seemed to be turning to their state government, at least in part, not because they know that it works, but because they are casting about for some part of government to which they can turn to restore at least part of their lost faith in the capacity of the U.S. national government. Over and over again, people seemed to be trying to convince themselves that the states must be better than Washington: They are closer to the people, so they must be able to do a better job of divining what the people want. Whether or not these hopes were objectively true was of little consequence to them.

This, of course, is not the whole story. Many of these interviewees do like Virginia for its own sake, or for aesthetic reasons, and these feelings were used by many of the interviewees to fill in the considerable gaps in their knowledge of the state's politics and government. The fact that people didn't seem to know much about their state government and its performance was no reason not to like that government. Instead, they felt confident about Richmond if they couldn't recall anything bad about it. The national government has the responsibility to take the lead in dealing with the nation's largest problems, and their capacities for handling those problems are there for all to see. Who expects Virginia's government to defeat al Qaeda, end a recession or bail out savings and loans that defaulted after squandering depositors' money? Washington is expected to solve these problems and is faulted for not handling them effectively. Richmond, in contrast, is not expected to manage such matters and is not blamed for being uninvolved. Many citizens interviewed here simply adored the state without giving much thought about what Virginia is doing or should be doing.

It is prudent at this point to raise once again the warning that the comments elicited in these interviews may not be transferrable outside this small study group. Likewise, things may be seen differently in the Old Dominion than in other states. Virginia has taken a leading role in making the case for decentralized governmental power throughout the twentieth century. Parents and teachers clearly have taken an active role in making children—particularly white children it seems—proud of their home state. The near universal love for Virginia among the white respondents attests to their success. Would people in other (Virginians might say "lesser") states love their own home states as much? Would they approach this alternative political order the same way? This study cannot say.

An important finding here is that one should not mistake this love of one's state for a belief that that state should have expanded powers. Many of the people who felt most positively about Virginia nevertheless felt that to give states more power might lead to disintegration of the national system, while even those frustrated with the performance of Virginia's government still were open to the idea of decentralizing some government functions. The interrelationships of these questions are far more complicated than is suggested by the ongoing debate in Washington over federalism.

One also should take note of further evidence of racial cleavages concerning public views on politics and government. While in earlier chapters African Americans seemed to have less of some types of political support than do whites, the discussions here suggest that the differences in views regarding Virginia are even greater than those regarding the national government.

These interviews also gave us new insights into the issue of interpersonal trust. As we have throughout this project, we find no clear pattern connecting the way one views human nature in general and the way one views government officials. People with negative views about human nature sometimes think that government officials are less trustworthy than ordinary folk, and they sometimes think they are more trustworthy. People with positive views likewise offer a variety of different comparisons involving ordinary people and government officials. These findings confirm the quantitative analysis of earlier chapters that suggested there was little correlation between interpersonal trust (as traditionally conceived) and feelings of political support.

Perhaps more important, though, these discussions give rise to the possibility that political science has not been focusing on interpersonal trust as effectively as it could be. While political trust has become a very popular area for inquiry in the wake of Putnam, the discussion here suggests that interpersonal trust as it is commonly conceived—that is, as one's general views concerning human nature—is inadequate for a full consideration of how people view others. These interviews suggest the need to consider a new type of trust, defined here as "community trust," that relates to how one views one's closest neighbors, people one has met face-to-face. This community trust is distinct from—and, in some cases, perhaps even directly opposed to—one's views concerning human nature overall. This may be the sort of trust that would allow for a full test of the "bowling alone" thesis and the ways that one's feelings about one's neighbors can affect one's political participation, one's democratic satisfaction and thereby, one's political support.

The people interviewed for this project have offered important insights concerning the ways in which citizens conceptualize interpersonal trust and alternative sovereignty of enhanced state power. The interviews suggest important avenues for further (and much more reliable) quantitative research into the issue of state power, which will be discussed in chapter 6. It is to this matter—and to the overall consideration of political support, both now and in the future—that this project now turns.

6

Conclusion

This final chapter has two major tasks. The first is to see whether the general enthusiasm that citizens have for state government really represents a thoughtful, viable alternative plan for the American political system. In particular, we will consider the extent to which feelings about the national and state governments are based on the actual performance of those governments, rather than on less substantive matters like the emotional, aesthetic attachments so much in evidence in the interviews in chapter 5. The second task is to summarize the nature of political support. What are the most important findings contained in this project? How do they relate to past ideas concerning political support? What are the implications of these findings for the state of political support in this country, both now and in the future? Along these same lines, we will consider new ways of looking at political support in future studies of this nature.

PUBLIC OPINION AND FEELINGS ABOUT STATE AND NATIONAL GOVERNMENTS

In the United States, the federal government and the state governments experience periods of increasing and decreasing influence over policymaking as well as times of waxing and waning citizen affections. Over the past decade, conditions seem to have improved for state governments on both counts. In recent years, leaders of both political parties have treated citizen feelings about state government as a significant force in national politics.

For the Republicans, Newt Gingrich's "Contract with America," with its focus on decentralized governmental authority, helped the Grand Old Party (GOP) take over both the U.S. House and the U.S. Senate in the

1994 midterm elections (Gingrich 1995; Jacobson 2001). During his presidential campaign in 1996, Bob Dole frequently cited the Tenth Amendment and promoted its "reserved" state-powers clause (Harris 1997). Even Democratic President Bill Clinton, who once proposed the government run a comprehensive national health care program, sought to seal his reelection in 1996 by accepting Republican plans to turn over to the states much of the control over the nation's welfare policy (Cammisa 1998). George W. Bush made a similar appeal for reduced national government authority during the 2000 presidential campaign (Ceaser and Busch 2001). This renewed interest in federalism by leaders of both political parties appears to be a prudent political strategy, because recent public opinion polls and in-depth interviews with citizens have shown considerable public enthusiasm for state governments and some discontent with the federal government (Craig 1993; Roeder 1994; Skocpol 1997). Along these same lines of politics, examinations of state voting patterns suggest a decoupling of federal and state political evaluations in elections over the past dozen years (Atkeson and Partin 1995; Niemi, Stanley and Vogel 1995).

Of course, as V.O. Key (1949) once observed, one's feelings about one's own state government may depend on factors that vary from jurisdiction to jurisdiction. Some states have greater capacity to perform public service functions than others. Some states have full-time legislatures and pay lawmakers professional salaries, for example, while in other states lawmakers are paid little and meet only briefly. Academic research suggests that states do tailor their public policies to match more precisely the wishes of their own distinct electorates (Erikson, Wright and McIver 1993). This pattern of state policy responsiveness can be found in a variety of issue areas, including abortion, civil rights, civic culture, economic policy and welfare (Berry and Berry 1992, 1994: Hill 1994; Hill, Leighley and Hinton-Andersson 1995; Rice and Sumberg 1997; Wetstein and Albritton 1995). In fact, public policy in states with citizen initiatives generally were not more responsive to public opinion than in states without them, largely because even the states without referenda were quite responsive to public opinion (Lascher, Hagen and Rochlin 1996).

The Data

The general public feelings regarding federalism were introduced in chapter 5 (see Table 5.1). To review, in the 1996 ANES, citizens first were asked to identify the level of government in which they had the most faith and confidence; the second question asked the respondent to say which level inspired the least faith and confidence. The federal government was the leading source of the least faith and confidence in 1996; 48 percent of the respondents had least faith and confidence in the national government, as compared to the 34 percent who selected the local level and the 19 percent who objected most to state government. The lack of enthusiasm for the federal government was roughly comparable to that of the mid-1970s, when trust fell greatly in the wake of the war in Vietnam and the Watergate scandal. (The question was not asked in the 2000 ANES.)

When citizens were asked about where they placed the greatest confidence, the pattern was reversed: The states finished first with 37 percent, as compared to 33 percent for local governments and 30 percent for the federal government. The idea of enhancing state governments apparently finds a ready audience of citizens, and one considerably enhanced from 1976, the last time these questions were asked in the ANES.

State governments were regarded much more highly in 1996 than they had been two decades earlier, as the controversial states' rights legacy of racial discrimination continues to fade from public consciousness with the passage of time. In addition, the increasing accountability and professionalization of many state governments in recent decades may have triggered changing—though not always positive—feelings about state government (Beyle 1993; Jewell 1982; Squire 1993).

This portion of the study also incorporates six measures not in the ANES that relate to the perceived responsiveness, performance and the culture of one's state government around the time of the 1996 survey. The first of these new measures, all of which are found in Appendix A, is a state partisan affinity variable that measures the extent to which the partisan composition of the lower chamber of each state legislature differed from the respondent's partisan leanings (U.S. Bureau of the Census 1997). Independents in states with a rough parity between the parties received low values, as did strong Republicans and Democrats in states where one's own party had large legislative majorities. Strong Democrats in states with large Republican-majority legislatures, and vice versa, had the highest values. These high values signify the greatest difference between an individual's personal preferences and the partisan composition of one's own state legislature. Residents of Nebraska, which has a nonpartisan legislature, were dropped from this analysis.

A second new state-performance variable measures the absolute distance between one's ideological position and state taxation per capita (U.S. Bureau of the Census 1997). Strong liberals in high-tax states conservatives in low-tax states and moderates in relatively moderately taxed states received low scores. Conservatives in high-tax states and liberals in low-tax states received the highest scores. This measure takes account of how close or how far one's personal preferences are from state policies in the highly salient issue area of tax policy.

The third measure this study uses is state populism, which ranks states on the extent to which they permit citizen initiative, referendum and recall of elected officials (Burns et al. 1993). A number of states have explicit mechanisms not found in the U.S. Constitution that allow citizens to become more directly involved in the policy-making process, including such things as citizen rights to use petitions to force recall elections for government officials and to place issues on the ballot (cf., Broder 2000).

The fourth state-specific measure is one of legislative professionalism, which measures the extent to which the legislature may have the institutional capacity to deal with more complicated issues (Patterson 1996).

The fifth measure is the state's average unemployment rate in 1996 (U.S. Bureau of the Census 1997). Unemployment is often seen as an important measure of governmental performance on the very important issue of economic performance (Wlezien 2001; Atkeson and Partin 1995).

The sixth measure provides for a test of the significance of state political cultures. Here we test whether residents of so-called moralistic states are more pro-national in orientation and whether citizens of the states designated "traditionalistic" and "individualistic" are more pro-state (Elazar 1972). The moralistic states are found generally in the country's northern tier and in the rural Midwest, areas where the national government has been regarded more positively. The traditionalistic states, generally found in the South (and a measure that includes all eleven states of the Confederacy), are less enthusiastic about the national government. The individualistic states are found largely in the Middle Atlantic and the industrial Midwest regions (Elazar 1972).

Results

Table 6.1 contains two logistic regressions testing the extent to which one's relative hostility toward either the federal government or one's own state government can be predicted by demographic, partisan and ideological measures and by political attitudes. The statistical technique we have used in several earlier chapters, OLS regression, is an improper approach for dichotomous dependent variables (was the respondent the most hostile toward the federal government in one instance and toward their own state government in the other). A straight-fitting OLS regression line does not fit logistic distributions, but a related technique, known as logistic regression, provides regression coefficients like those in OLS regression and, therefore, results that will look somewhat familiar to those found in OLS regression equations. One key difference between the two techniques is that the effectiveness of the overall model in logistic regression can be measured both by an r-square statistic and by the percentage of the cases predicted correctly. Table 6.1 contains unstandardized coefficients, an r-square measure and case-classification results for those two logistic regressions.

Table 6.1

Faith and Confidence in Federal and State Governments: Logistic Regression Analyses

1996	National (b)	State (b)
Education	-.04	.05
Income	-.13	-.01
Sex	-.06	-.02
Race	-.38	.31
Party Identification	-.27***	.16**
Ideology	-.13*	.17*
No Care	.16*	.003
No Say	.10	-.10
Complex	.10	-.04
Economy Past Year	.24*	-.26*
Populism	.13	.01
Professionalism	.05	-.26
Unemployment	.07	.04
Partisan Affinity	.005	-.01
Taxation Affinity	.000	.000
Moralistic	-.26**	.09
N	979	979
-2 Log Likelihood	1187.226	863.663
Cox/Snell r-square	.159	.070

* $p < .05$ ** $p < .01$ *** $p < .001$

Notes: Coefficients are unstandardized. Cut value for the "National" dependent variable was set at .48, since 48 percent of respondents had the least faith and confidence in the national government. Cut value for "State" dependent variable was set at .19, since 19 percent were least favorably disposed to that level of government.

With respect to the results relating to the federal government, one notices at first the powerful influence played by party identification and, to a lesser extent, ideology. Liberals and Democrats were disposed the most positively toward the federal government, as one would expect. Other influential measures in this model included those of efficacy ("no

(Table 6.1 continued)

Classification: Predicted versus Observed Preference—Federal

	Predicted Least	Predicted Not Least	Percent Correct
Observed Least	313	173	64.4%
Observed Not Least	147	346	70.2%
TOTAL Percent Correct			67.3%

Classification: Predicted versus Observed Preference—State

	Predicted Least	Predicted Not Least	Percent Correct
Observed Least	0	180	0%
Observed Not Least	0	799	100%
TOTAL Percent Correct			81.6%

care") and how positively one viewed the economy's performance over the past year. The federal model, which has a Cox/Snell r-square of .159, correctly predicts 67.3 percent of the cases: 64.4 percent of the cases where the federal government was liked least and 70.2 percent of the cases where Washington was not the least liked.

Only one state-specific measure showed a statistically significant relationship with feelings about the federal government: whether the state was classified as moralistic. In a departure from what was hypothesized, the more moralistic the state, the more likely a resident was to be critical of the federal government, a result, perhaps, of the shrinking policy role Washington sought for itself in 1995 and 1996, around the time this survey was conducted.

The right column uses the same independent variables to predict an individual's hostility toward his or her own state government (Pearson's $r = -.46$ for the two dependent variables used in the two models reported in Table 6.1). Although the state model has a higher overall prediction rate, 81.6 percent, this is a highly misleading statistic; the high percentage comes from the fact that the model does not effectively distinguish people relatively hostile toward state governments from those more hostile toward some other level of government. The Cox/Snell r-square reading of .07 demonstrates the fundamental weakness of the state model, as does a closer look at the classification pattern.

Even so, many of the same independent variables were influential in both the federal and state models. Strong Republicans, conservatives and those who evaluated the economy's recent performance more negatively were most likely to feel positively about state government. Strangely, not one of the six state-specific measures had a statistically significant relationship with individual feelings about state government, even though the measures were designed to elicit state government evaluations explicitly.

Why might the differences between predictions in the left and right sides of Table 6.1 be so dramatic? Democratic citizens seem far more committed to a positive evaluation of the federal government than Republicans to a positive evaluation of the state governments. After all, Republican ideas of reducing federal power can be, and sometimes are, coupled with proposals to reduce state government authority as well.

The results here suggest that support for one's own state government does not spring largely from frustration with the federal government. People generally do not turn to their state capitals because of a sense that Washington doesn't care about them, though economic matters do have some relevance to one's feelings about federalism. One's feelings about one's state government has even less to do with the state-specific measures: the professionalism, the partisan or taxation affinity found in one's own state. Broad orientations toward the political world like partisanship and ideology proved much more important for predicting support for state government than any substantive evaluation of what one's own state government has or has not done. Taken together, these findings suggest that rhetoric, not results, is driving public opinion in the direction of state governments and away from the national government.

In addition, the results demonstrate that Democrats have done a better job in inculcating the values of big government among their loyalists than the Republicans have in convincing their own supporters of the dangers of big government. The findings in Table 6.1 are consistent with the New Deal and Great Society traditions of the Democratic party, as well as with the pronouncements by the Republicans—especially by Gingrich in the 1990s and in the 1996 presidential campaign by Bob Dole himself—about the evils of an overly centralized government. It may be harder to criticize one level of government and sing the virtues of another than some Republicans thought.

Is Enhanced State Power a Viable Alternative System?

These results offer little encouragement for those who believe that satisfaction with government can be revived by taking power away from the national government and giving it to the states. Although there are those with strong ideological aversions to national government power, many of these same people are skeptical about state government power as well. And the Democrats appear to have done a far better job of convincing their partisans of the advantages of a strong national government than the Republicans have done of convincing their partisans of the advantages of a strong state government. The relative weakness of the state government model may be due partially to the fact that opinions might have been more consistent regarding one federal government than fifty different state governments. Even so, most of the state-specific measures added to this study did not improve the predictive power of the government preference models in Table 6.1.

If opinions about state government are largely ideological and partisan in orientation, they are more the result of what the politicians have been saying than what the state governments themselves actually have been doing. Support for state governments does not spring from performance shortcomings on the part of the federal government. Nor do positive feelings about state governments correspond to a given's state's actual performance or even to its political culture.

One also can wonder whether citizens who dislike federal government power may also dislike state government power. The state questions used here, though a dramatic improvement on what has been available in past surveys, may force respondents to choose which government they like the most even if they dislike them all intensely. To deal with this potential problem, future surveys might use thermometer measures, or at least a 5-point like/dislike scale to tap more precisely citizen orientations toward the different governments.

This quantitative test of how feelings about state government affect one's political support offers a limited test of some of the issues raised by those voices of federalism heard in chapter 5. Since 1996 came during a period of relative hostility toward the federal government, this study cannot say whether these patterns among issues would be similar in 2000, or after the terrorist attacks of 2001. After all, the ANES returned to its comparative evaluations of governments questions in 1996 after a twenty-year hiatus (but dropped them again in the 2000 survey). Further research into the changing nature of comparative evaluations of government and politics over time also should be an important part of future research. We do not yet know whether a revived states' rights doctrine will remain prominent in the minds of voters and candidates in the years to come. If it does, future surveys should examine whether the basic orientations toward the state and federal governments begin to correspond more directly to the actual performance of one's own state government.

RETURNING TO POLITICAL SUPPORT AND POLITICAL CRISIS

In normal circumstances, public opinion in the United States has been described as a glass half empty (Huntington 1981). Americans do not accept easily government performance as adequate, and citizens at all levels of education and of all ideologies can find things for which to criticize the country. The Framers, of course, would not have had it any other way. The U.S. political system depends on a muscular, skeptical public oversight of political figures who compete with one another for the affections of citizens. This is true both within the national government, as seen through the many conflicts between the legislative and executive branches, and among the governments of the various levels, as seen through the many battles between the national government and the various states. Every government official is thought to have an incentive to try to become the public's favorite, and the public is thought to be the chief beneficiary of this competition.

In normal circumstances, citizens are not particularly inclined to see what is working about America, rather, they are quick to find things about this country that dissatisfy them. In a country where even thirty-year veterans of the Washington political environment try to campaign as outsiders (as Bob Dole did during his failed campaign for president in 1996), it is quite clear that the national government is not held in particularly high regard.

Of course different people are angry at different things. Republicans may be angry at the Democratic filibusters in the U.S. Senate and Democrats may be angry at the Republican majority in the U.S. House and Senate, but these differences go far deeper than that. Presidents are expected above all to provide solid performance in certain public policy areas, most notably the economy and issues of war and peace. Congress is not held to such a high standard on policy matters, but it is held to a far higher standard than is the nation's chief executive in terms of both the legislative branch's responsiveness to public opinion and its general trustworthiness. Likewise, distinct patterns of political support that vary by age presented earlier in this project demonstrate the wide range of reasons for citizen frustration with government.

Do These Public Opinions Add Up to a Regime Crisis?

Some political scientists have said that it is hard to see precisely how important this citizen discontent is, since the system seems more or less to be surviving reasonably well in spite of apparent recent declines in political support (cf., Craig 1993; Parker 1986; Stewart 1986). While conditions of political support in the United States do not appear to have fallen to the level where we should be questioning whether or not our system is in imminent danger of internal collapse, the widespread frustration of recent years certainly gives us reason to focus on possible internal threats to the stability of our political order (Craig 1993; Weatherford 1987). While the 2001 terrorist attacks on the United States has been seen widely as "changing everything," the evidence from public polls demonstrates that, for most citizens, concerns of terrorism quickly became a matter of secondary importance behind that of economic matters. Within a matter of months, a sluggish overall economy, corporate fraud and deep declines in the financial markets became greater citizen concerns than terrorism (Stevenson and Elder 2002; Kohut 2002). Of course, even for those who believe that America has been brought together by this tragedy, the deaths of 3,000 Americans is a dreadfully high price to pay for the restoration of political support. And, hopefully, it is not one we will have to pay ever again.

Clearly, then, people looking at questions of political support should not be pacified by the outpouring of patriotism seen in the wake of the terrorist attacks. Indeed, a number of civil libertarians have expressed concerns that the fear of terrorism may make citizens too acquiescent, allowing the government to intrude too far into areas of constitutional rights (Fainaru and Eggen 2002; Pierre 2002). Indeed, even the lawmakers who are investigating intelligence agencies' handling of evidence that might have provided an early warning of the attacks to come are themselves being subject to FBI investigations (Priest and Dewar 2002).

The political support troubles catalogued here are consistent with many of the troubles seen by those scholars looking at legitimation crises faced by other advanced Western societies. As any government's responsibilities grow and become more varied, it becomes increasingly difficult for public officials to manage activities further and further removed from government's competence and capabilities (Easton 1965b; Habermas 1973; Offe 1984; Held 1987). As citizen demands increase, government is thought to have to intervene more and more in the operations of a culture, both through the provision of social welfare benefits and through the collection of sufficient resources to finance such programs. Yet increased government takings can trigger resentment even if the programs are regarded as well-run, and recent Republican national campaigns, marked by promises to lower taxes, may trigger declines in the amount of money distributed in the programs, as well as the amount spent on oversight (Ceaser and Busch 1997, 2001). Of course, when governments try to handle these more controversial issues, governments are likely to be criticized for their mistakes no matter how well or how poorly they do. These mistakes are as much a result of having to deal with controversial social welfare functions that are outside the government's traditional expertise as anything else, yet the public demands such programs. Programs like welfare are immensely difficult to manage (How much is enough? How much is too much?), and they likely always will be controversial because such programs are inherently more divisive than a debate over the relative merits of a strong economy versus a weak one.

Given the fact that government does many things that at least *someone* will object to, it should come as no surprise that citizens use a wide variety of measures to evaluate the U.S. government and its component parts. For some people, the government's economic performance is a key, if not *the* key, measure. For others, the government's performance is graded primarily on military preparedness. For still others, the extent to which government officials could be trusted is the salient issue. And, even if people use one of these measures to evaluate Congress, there is no assurance they use the same measure to evaluate the president.

Bubbling throughout the citizen evaluations of government presented in these chapters, however, was the issue of whether the government pays enough attention to ordinary people when it sets policy. The generational and racial differences found here demonstrate the wide variety of needs that the national government must address simultaneously to maintain widespread political support. While the United States clearly has not traveled as far down the road toward providing a generous social benefit system comparable to that provided by many western European nations, the U.S. government nevertheless faces the difficult challenge of trying to satisfy spiraling citizen demands without bankrupting its economy and/or angering politically influential elites (Drew 2002; Greider 1992; Held 1987).

This brings us to the central paradox of American politics: Citizens have powerful and fervently held ideals but do not want a national government to be strong enough or efficient enough to carry them out effectively (Huntington 1981). While more than two centuries of political criticism in the United States demonstrates that there is often a powerful force opposing centralized American governmental power, this study demonstrates that many citizens do not appear to accept this contradiction. They may not want a very efficient government, but the results here indicate that they want at least a competent one. How Americans feel about the president, the members of Congress and even members of the Supreme Court depends largely on how well these officials have performed on the issues citizens care about and whether they are listening to citizens. The evidence in this study shows that, American skepticism of centralized government notwithstanding, citizens may feel that government in recent years has become too inefficient. The results of the 1992 and 1994 national elections—which resulted in the widespread rejection of an incumbent Republican president and, two years later, of incumbent Democratic majorities in the U.S. House and the U.S. Senate—also speak to the pervasive frustration with government that was found in this study of political support.

When we consider younger citizens and African Americans, two groups whose members tended to have relatively low political support, the severity of our nation's crisis of confidence becomes more apparent. The diversity of our nation can lend itself to deep divisions, which, of course, works against any quick or easy resolution of citizen differences (Citrin 1996). The fact that citizens from the Baby Boom and the Next generations usually had the lowest levels of political support suggests that efforts to maintain if not revive political support among citizens 50 years of age and younger should be a priority. Restoring the confidence of these younger adults is likely to be particularly difficult since contemporary demands on government tend to involve the hardest issues for governments to satisfy.

An equally troublesome finding is that African American citizens generally had lower levels of political support than Whites. This distinct support pattern occurs despite the national government's efforts over the past several decades to combat discrimination in government, education and business. These racial disparities in political support tended to be pronounced more among the youngest African Americans, another indication that political support problems may intensify in the years ahead.

Responding to Citizen Discontent: Weakening the National Government?

American public frustration with government is not very significant, according to some researchers, because most Americans could not think of a better country than the United States if asked to do so. Even in the northern California of the 1970s, a part of the country (and a time) well known for its alternative political and cultural orientations, very few people were willing to rank another country above United States (Sniderman 1981). With no widely recognized alternative vision of political authority filling the minds of citizens, the existing American political regime was quite secure, researchers concluded more than two decades ago.

But researchers might have been looking in the wrong place, or perhaps to the wrong time, for an alternative plan for political authority in

America. The Fredericksburg area interviews involved several people who would prefer an alternative sovereignty: enhanced state power and reduced federal power. The interviews are hardly sufficient enough to settle these differences, but two national survey questions asking about relative rankings for national, state and local government did indicate that enhanced state power is a vision that many Americans could embrace. This alternative political model is not all that unfamiliar, after all, since the rise of a powerful peacetime national government did not occur until the New Deal, until after our country had marked its 150th birthday.

Paul M. Sniderman (1981) suggested that one cannot compare something to nothing. Well, the alternative order discussed in the Fredericksburg area interviews proved to be useful just as Sniderman predicted: by providing a means of comparison for evaluating the status quo. While the people interviewed here usually had very vague images of state government, the important finding here is that their opinions about state government—whether positive or negative—were held strongly and affected the way they felt about the national government. While there was some evidence based on the limited survey questions asked of the interviewees that indicated that the interview sample was quite polarized on the merits of greater state power, interviewees often used this alternative vision to help them assess the Washington-dominant status quo when engaged in an in-depth discussion of the topic.

These opinions, strong as they might have been among the interviewees and those people surveyed in the 1996 ANES, were based primarily on opinion, not performance. As Table 6.1 demonstrates, enthusiasm for state power is based primarily on ideology and has little to do with any real understanding of how well state governments handle their existing responsibilities. It is a slim reed indeed on which to rest this country's future. Before a plan to give state governments more power can be endorsed, a far more effective public analysis of the capabilities and performances of state governments should be undertaken. Once new evaluations of state performance begin to appear, state governments may not be the panacea that they appear to some.

The difference between findings by earlier researchers (cf., Sniderman 1981) and the interviews and survey analyses conducted in this chapter and the preceding one represent an interesting distinction worth considering in more depth and breadth than has been possible with the available interviews and data. Whether the patterns seen in this small sample of Fredericksburg area citizens are repeated in the nation at large, or whether most people continue to lack an alternative vision of government, is a very important question for another day. And whether the analysis of voter orientations toward state governments in 2000 or 2004 would yield the same findings as the analysis of voters in 1996 is impossible to say.

Interpersonal Trust: Rebuilding the Tie that Binds?

This study contains some evidence in support of the ideas of Robert Putnam (2000) concerning the ways in which interpersonal trust may relate to public feelings about government. Interpersonal trust seems not to matter in terms of one's level of overall democratic satisfaction, but, in some cases, there was a relationship between how negatively one felt about other people and how negatively one felt about Congress. On balance, though, interpersonal trust measures did not seem to matter a great deal in the quantitative analysis of political support.

While there seemed to be little relationship between interpersonal trust, which relates to one's general views of human nature, and political support or democratic satisfaction, there seems to be an important level of "community trust," the trust one feels for one's neighbors or those people with whom one interacts face-to-face. The interviews suggested that Putnam's theories may be more applicable to this community trust. Unfortunately, because this is a new idea about the nature of trust, we need to engage in the cumbersome, tedious business of trying out new questions for future mass surveys of public opinion. Only then will the "bowling alone" thesis receive the full test it deserves.

The Bottom Line

Is America in the midst of a political support crisis? The overall answer is "yes": Citizens have been getting angrier at and more dissatisfied with government over the past several decades. Some of the trends shown here demonstrate that our civic connections are becoming increasingly frayed. As trust, efficacy, perceived governmental responsiveness and governmental competence weaken, citizens view their political system more negatively.

Citizen frustrations with government have important consequences. Government officials and political scientists should not simply dismiss the importance of the long-term declines in political trust as a natural part of an American antiauthority ethos. As the public's mistrust of government has increased in recent decades, citizens under normal circumstances are less likely to give the national government latitude to do what it believes is best. And even abnormal circumstances do not always generate long-term changes in citizen priorities and orientations, as the evidence so far following the 2001 terrorist attacks indicates. Prospects for a long-term reversal of fortune on political system trust are not particularly bright.

While any changes in citizens' basic attachments to government are likely to come slowly, the measures of declining trust, declining political participation and decreased legitimacy for elected officials can lead to a decreased ability on the part of our political system to handle and perhaps to withstand some future incident that causes severe strain on this nation.

While long-term trends in political support are difficult to determine through the survey information available, the generational and racial cleavages and increasing youth cynicism found in these surveys suggest that support for the national government seems more likely to decline than rise as time passes and as the more positively disposed older citizens fade from the scene. Even prolonged economic good times may not be sufficient to restore citizens' faith and trust in government, particularly among younger citizens, given their concerns about both the way government behaves and what policies government pursues (Inglehart 1990). Age and racial divisions represent clear fault lines in American politics, ones not easily bridged by crosscutting cleavages. These differences therefore represent important warnings for the future of political support.

FUTURE RESEARCH

Much remains for future projects that will consider further the issues surrounding political support. In particular, it would be useful to examine more explicitly the amount of latitude that citizens choose to give government: a little (through term limits, balanced budget amendments and greater direct democracy) or a lot (through giving government more discretion to "do the right thing"). This area seems particularly important in the wake of the concerns being raised over questionable governmental conduct in the holding of people in custody in the wake of the 2001 terrorist attacks. Indeed, it would be very useful to plot the trajectory of public feelings on this score and see whether some generational groups are more inclined to give the government greater latitude than others are. Although the evidence so far suggests that public frustration has moved quickly back to its pre-attack levels, this crisis may have the makings of a particularly important impressionable-years event in the life of today's twenty-somethings. Although the events of that horrible day shocked all Americans, it could have a particularly powerful long-term socializing effect on today's adults. If that occurs, the ripples of that event could be felt for the next several decades. This incident and its aftermath could be a key socializing effect that remains influential for decades. Although the preliminary evidence suggested this may not be likely, the effects of September 11 on today's young Americans could turn out to be on a par with the powerful effects that the Depression, World War II and Vietnam had in creating the political orientations of older genera-tions.

Some of the most important and dramatic findings in this project in-volved the differences among generational groups and between Blacks and Whites in their political support and the factors that explained the levels of support for individuals in different groups. Further investiga-tion in these areas also may be a productive project, particularly in the study of youth orientations toward politics. The future is found in the Next generation, and their orientations found in this analysis demand more extensive analysis as this birth cohort grows into greater political prominence.

Further consideration of state governments also is warranted, given the apparent popularity among some citizens for transferring some fed-eral responsibilities to the states. The preliminary indications from the Fredericksburg area interviews are that people adopted this position without much evaluation of state governments or awareness of the states' current responsibilities or competence. Instead, it seemed that people felt that Richmond had to be more responsible and less corrupt than Washington. There might even be a form of political schizophrenia in Virginia with respect to citizen evaluations of Richmond and Wash-ington. Political science may consider more extensively feelings about state governments and how they may relate to political support on a national level. This project really could not do much more with the ap-parent fondness for state governments than simply observe the trend and note that it did not seem based upon any evidence of state government performance.

Another major issue to be considered further in light of these findings is this idea of community trust, or trust of those people with whom one deals face-to-face. The preliminary results of the interview section of this project suggest that a major reconsideration of the interpersonal trust concept may be in order. Clearly, much larger investigations than the Fredericksburg area interviews used here, especially large-sample sur-veys, are needed to determine to what extent the preliminary findings found in chapter 5 and earlier in this chapter can be replicated.

Appendix C, which contains a variety of questions relating to these different types of trust, would be a good place to start in a more exten-sive study of the different kinds of personal and political trust. The ques-tion of how many neighbors one would let borrow their television sets elicited a variety of interesting responses that suggest the presence of two types of interpersonal trust: general views concerning human nature and community trust. That question could be applied to other people, including political figures: "Would you let the governor borrow your television set if he or she lived on your street? How about Bill Clinton? How about George W. Bush?" Other possible questions that could tap community trust would be whether respondents wish they knew their neighbors better and whether they would trust them to walk their dogs or feed their cats if they had to go out of town suddenly.

Along these same lines, a series of questions used in some of the interviews elicited some interesting distinctions among the types of trust. Citizens were asked in interviews to describe their basic views of human nature. They then were asked whether they considered politicians more trustworthy, less trustworthy or as trustworthy when compared to ordinary citizens. This question also could be asked about one's neighbors, and perhaps about state and national officials, to establish a battery of questions that would allow for a more direct comparison of these different kinds of trust along very similar measures.

A much more extensive search for distinctions among these types of trust would allow for a much more effective test of the importance of community trust in the construction of public attachments to the political order (Putnam 2000). While this project found that views of human nature did not matter much for levels of political support, the very different issue of community trust (once we have learned to measure it effectively) may be much more relevant to political support.

The most important area for subsequent studies to consider, however, is the trajectory of political support. Because of the one-time or few-times availability of many of these measures, any discussion in this project of across-time changes is quite speculative. While things like generational differences may offer an indication of future trends, one would be on very thin ice to predict all that definitively about subsequent developments.

A FINAL THOUGHT

Representative democracy is a difficult proposition. With modern polling and communication techniques, policy makers have more information than ever before about what citizens want. The problem, at least for some policy makers, is that citizens also have much more information, about both what they want and exactly what their elected officials are doing in Washington. This can lead to a more responsive government, or it can lead to more cynical citizens. To restore the nation to political health, to increase the volume in the reservoir of political support, government officials have to pay much closer attention to citizen demands of government; public officials must behave in ways that encourage citizens to trust them and to believe that their own voices will be heard by policy makers who are competent enough to do the job of representing their fellow citizens. Above all, political figures need to act in ways that can help make ordinary citizens proud of America and that can help convince this country's long-suffering citizens that government officials are listening and are taking citizen views seriously in public policy-making. Too often citizens believe the national government does not care, and public feelings about that government suffer accordingly.

APPENDIX A

American National Elections Study Survey Questions

Questions in Appendix A are from the American National Elections Studies unless otherwise noted. Recoding as well as differences in question wording and response coding in different years are discussed following the response choices, where applicable. All questions were not asked in all years. All variables were recoded so that the most civically positive response (e.g., the most trusting of government) is scored highest.

MEDIA USE

NETWORK How many days in the past week did you watch the national network news on TV? (0 to 7 days).

PAPER How many days in the past week did you read a daily newspaper? (0 to 7 days).

BACKGROUND

INCOME Family income in 1999 before taxes. 01. Zero–$4,999; 02. $5,000–9,999; 03. $10,000–$14,999; 04. $15,000–$24,999; 05. $25,000–$34,999; 06. $35,000–$49,999; 07. $50,000–$64,999; 08. $65,000–$74,999; 09. $75,000–$84,999; 10. $85,000–$94,999; 11. $95,000–$104,999; 12. $105,000–$114,999; 13. $115,000–$124,999; 14. $125,000–$134,999; 15. $135,000–$144,999; 16. $145,000–$154,999; 17. $155,000–$164,999; 18. $165,000–$174,999; 19. $175,000–$184,999; 20. $185,000–$194,999; 21. $195,000–$199,999; 22. $200,000 and over.

PARTY IDENTIFICATION (ID) 0. STRONG DEMOCRAT.......

6. STRONG REPUBLICAN (Folded to measure intensity of partisan feelings: 0=4, 6=4, 1=3, 5=3, 2=2, 4=2, 3=1.)

IDEOLOGY   1. EXTREMELY LIBERAL.......7. EXTREMELY CONSERVATIVE (Folded to measure intensity of ideology: 1=4, 7=4, 2=3, 6=3, 3=2, 5=2, 4=1, 0=0.)

EDUCATION   01. 8 grades or less; 02. 9–11 grades, no further schooling (includes 12 years without diploma or equivalency); 03. High school diploma, or equivalency test; 04. More than 12 years of schooling, no higher degree; 05. Junior or community college level degrees (Associate degrees); 06. Bachelor's level degrees; 17+ years, no advanced degree; 07. Advanced degree, including law degree.

GENERATION   G.I. Generation (born 1901–1924); Silent Generation (born 1925–1942); Baby Boomers (born 1943–1960); Next Generation (born 1961–1981).

SEX   1. Male; 2. Female.

RACE   1. White 2. African American (rest missing)

POLITICAL TRUST INDEX (Four variable index for 2000, alpha = .63)

TRUSTDC   How much of the time do you think you can trust the government in Washington to do what is right—just about always, most of the time, or only some of the time?

WASTE   Do you think that people in government waste a lot of the money we pay in taxes, waste some of it, or don't waste very much of it?

BIG INTERESTS   Would you say the government is pretty much run by a few big interests looking out for themselves or that it is run for the benefit of all the people?

CROOKED   Do you think that quite a few of the people running the government are crooked, not very many are, or do you think hardly any of them are crooked?

POLITICAL EFFICACY INDEX (Three variable index for 2000, alpha = .61)

NO SAY   <Respondent agrees/disagrees that ... > People like me don't have any say about what the government does. (Agree Strongly; Agree Somewhat; Neither Agree nor Disagree; Disagree Somewhat; Disagree Strongly)

NO CARE <Respondent agrees/disagrees that ... > Public officials don't care much about what people like me think. (Options as in NO SAY)

COMPLEX <Respondent agrees/disagrees that ... > Sometimes politics and government seem so complicated that a person like me can't really understand what's going on. (Options as in NO SAY)

GOVERNMENTAL COMPETENCE (No index possible for 2000)

U.S. WORLD POSITION During the past year, would you say that the United States' position in the world has grown weaker, stayed about the same, or has it grown stronger?

ECONOMY PAST YEAR How about the economy? Would you say that over the past year the nation's economy has gotten better, stayed about the same, or gotten worse? (If better) Would you say much better or somewhat better? (If worse) Would you say much worse or somewhat worse?

ECONOMY NEXT YEAR What about the next 12 months? Do you expect the national economy to get better, get worse, or stay about the same? (If better) Would you say much better or somewhat better? (If worse) Would you say much worse or somewhat worse?

GOVERNMENTAL RESPONSIVENESS INDEX (Two variable index for 2000; alpha = .61)

GOVERNMENT LISTEN Over the years, how much attention do you feel the government pays to what people think when it decides what to do—a good deal, some, or not much?

ELECTIONS LISTEN How much do you feel that having elections makes the government pay attention to what the people think—a good deal, some, or not much?

INTERPERSONAL TRUST INDEX (Four variable index for 2000; alpha = .53)

PEOPLE HELPFUL Would you say that most people would take advantage of you if they had the chance, or would they try to be fair?

TRUST PEOPLE Generally speaking, would you say that most people can be trusted, or that you can't be too careful in dealing with people?

VOLUNTEER Many people say they have less time these days to do volunteer work. What about you, were you able to devote any time to volunteer work in the last 12 months?

JURY   If you were selected to serve on a jury, would you be happy to do it, or would you rather not serve?

FEDERALISM   (Questions not asked in 2000 ANES)

LEVEL MOST   We find that people differ in how much faith and confidence they have in various levels of government in this country. In your case, do you have more faith and confidence in national government, the government of this state, or in the local government around here?

LEVEL LEAST   Which level of government do you have the least faith and confidence in: the national government, the government of this state, or the local government around here?

STATE PREFERENCE   (Combines the responses to the above two federalism measures) 01. State least favored, federal most favored; 02. State least favored, federal middle (local government most favored); 03. State middle, federal most; 04. State middle, federal least; 05. State most, federal middle; 06. State most, federal least.

POLITICAL SYSTEM EVALUATIONS

DEMOCRATIC SATISFACTION   On the whole, are you satisfied, fairly satisfied, not very satisfied, or not at all satisfied, with the way democracy works in the United States?

FAIR ELECTIONS   In some countries people believe their elections are conducted fairly. In other countries, people believe that their elections are conducted unfairly. Thinking of the last election in the United States, where would you place it on this scale of one to five where one means that the last election was conducted fairly and five means that the last election was conducted unfairly.

FEDERAL THERMOMETER   0–100 overall rating for the federal government.

CLINTON THERMOMETER   0–100 overall rating for Bill Clinton.

CONGRESS THERMOMETER   0–100 overall rating for Congress.

SUPREME COURT THERMOMETER   0–100 overall rating for the Supreme Court.

STATE PREFERENCE VARIABLES (NOT FROM ANES)

POPULISM (0–3 scale).   Does state offer citizen initiative, citizen referendum, and citizen recall? [Source: Burns et al. 1993]

PROFESSIONALISM   Citizen, hybrid, or professional state legislature?
[Source: Patterson 1996]

UNEMPLOYMENT   The state unemployment rate (1996 average).
[Source: *U.S. Bureau of the Census* 1997]

PARTISAN AFFINITY   The absolute partisan distance between an individual and the lower chamber of the state legislature before the 1996
elections. The seven-point party identification scale was spread along the
range of level of GOP control. [Source: *U.S. Bureau of the Census* 1997]

TAXATION AFFINITY   The absolute ideological distance between an
individual and his or her state government's tax collections per capita.
[Source: *U.S. Bureau of the Census* 1997]

MORALISTIC   Pure moralistic states (n = 9) scored a 3; moralistic dom-
inant states (n = 8) scored a 2; states with a strong moralistic strain (n
= 10) scored a 1; states without a strong moralistic strain (n = 23) scored
a zero. [Source: Elazar 1972]

APPENDIX B

Hibbing and Theiss-Morse Survey Questions

INDEPENDENT VARIABLES

BACKGROUND

RACE   What race do you consider yourself?

1. White/Caucasian. . . . 3. Black/African American. . . . 6. Other (coded missing)

INCOME   I am going to mention a number of income categories. When I come to the category that describes your total household income before taxes in 1991, please stop me.

1. Under 5 thousand (0–4,999)
2. 5 to 10 thousand (5,000–9,999)
3. 10 to 15 thousand (10,000–14,999)
4. 15 to 20 thousand (15,000–19,999)
5. 20 to 25 thousand (20,000–24,999)
6. 25 to 30 thousand (25,000–29,999)
7. 30 to 35 thousand (30,000–34,999)
8. 35 to 40 thousand (35,000–39,999)
9. 40 to 50 thousand (40,000–49,999)
11. 50 to 60 thousand (50,000–59,999)
13. 60 to 70 thousand (60,000–69,999)
15. 75 to 100 thousand (75,000–99,999)
20. 100 thousand or more (100,000 +)
99. Don't know [DK], Refused (coded missing)

EDUCATION   What is the highest level of school you have completed?

1. Less than high school
2. Some high school
3. High school graduate
4. Some technical school
5. Technical school graduate
6. Some college
7. College graduate
8. Post graduate or professional degree
9. Other; DK; Refused (coded missing)

BIRTH YEAR　Respondent's year of birth (Recoded as AGE).

PARTY IDENTIFICATION (ID)　Generally speaking, do you usually think of yourself as a Democrat, a Republican, an Independent, or something else? (If Independent) Do you think of yourself as closer to the Republican or Democratic party? (If D/R) Would you call yourself a strong Democrat (or Republican) or not a very strong Democrat (or Republican)?

1. Strong Democrat
2. Not a Strong Democrat
3. Independent leaning Democrat
4. Independent
5. Independent leaning Republican
6. Not a Strong Republican
7. Strong Republican
9. Refused; Something Else (coded missing)

FOLDED PARTY ID　The party identification scale is recoded to measure intensity of partisan feelings: 7,1=4; 6,2=3, 5,3=2; 4=1.

IDEOLOGY　We hear a lot of talk these days about liberals and conservatives. Do you consider yourself liberal, slightly liberal, moderate, slightly conservative, or conservative?

1. Liberal
2. Slightly liberal
3. Moderate
4. Slightly conservative
5. Conservative
6. Don't Know (DK); Refused

FOLDED IDEOLOGY　The ideology scale is recoded to measure intensity of ideology: 5,1=3; 4,2=2; 6,3=1.

SEX　1. Male　　2. Female

PATRIOTISM

PROUD CONGRESS　Have members of Congress ever made you feel proud?

1. Yes　2. No　3. DK; Refused (coded missing)
(Recoded: 2=1, 1=2).

PROUD　Which makes you feel most proud?

1. Supreme Court justices　2. President　3. Members of Congress
4. All　　　　　　　　　　5. None　　6. DK; Refused (coded missing)
(Recoded for intensity of pride: 4=2; 1,2,3=1; 5=0).

FAIR OUTCOMES　How satisfied are you with the fairness of the policies that the U.S. Congress passes? Are you very satisfied, somewhat satisfied, somewhat dissatisfied, or very dissatisfied?

1. Very satisfied   2. Somewhat satisfied   3. Not very satisfied
4. Not at all satisfied   5. Neutral   6. DK; Refused (coded missing)

(Recoded: 4=1, 3=2, 5=3, 2=4, 1=5).

POLITICAL SYSTEM TRUST

ORDINARY PEOPLE   Congress is too far removed from ordinary people.

1. Strongly agree   2. Agree   3. Disagree
4. Strongly disagree   5. Neutral   6. DK; Refused (coded missing)
(Recoded: 1=1, 2=2, 3=4, 4=5, 5=3).

INTEREST INFLUENCE   Congress is too heavily influenced by interest groups when making decisions.

1. Strongly agree   2. Agree   3. Disagree
4. Strongly disagree   5. Neutral   6. DK; Refused (coded missing)
(Recoded: 1=1, 2=2, 3=4, 4=5, 5=3).

POLITICAL EFFICACY

COMPLEX   Sometimes politics and government seem so complicated that a person like me can't understand what's going on.

1. Agree   2. Disagree
3. Don't know   4. Refused (coded missing)
(Recoded: 1=1, 2=3, 3=2).

NO CARE   I don't think public officials care much about what people like me think. [options and recoding as above]

NO SAY   People like me don't have any say about what the government does. [options and recoding as above]

VOTE SAY   Voting is the only way people like me can have any say about how the government runs things. [options and recoding as above]

GOVERNMENTAL COMPETENCE

CONGRESS COMPETENT   How good a job is the U.S. Congress doing in dealing with this (previously identified by Respondent [R] as the nation's most important) problem, a good job, a fair job, or a poor job?

1. Good job   2. Fair job   3. Poor job

4. Inappropriate—doesn't deal with problem   5. DK; Refused
                                                            (coded miss-
                                                            ing)

(Recoded: 1=3, 2=2, 3=1, 4—missing).

PRESIDENT COMPETENT   How good a job is the President doing in dealing with this problem, a good, fair, or poor job?

[options and recoding as above]

COURT COMPETENT   How good a job is the U.S. Supreme Court doing in dealing with this problem, a good, fair, or poor job?

[options and recoding as above]

MEDIA USE

NEWS SOURCE   I'd like to ask where you usually get most of your news about what's going on in the world today—is it from the newspapers, radio, television, magazines, or talking with others?

1. Newspapers   2. Radio   3. Television

4. Magazines (coded   5. Talking with others   6. DK; Refused (coded miss-
missing)   (coded missing)   ing)

TV USE   How many days in the past week did you watch the news on TV?

0–7. Number of days   9. DK; Refused (coded missing)

PAPER USE   How many days in the past week did you read a daily newspaper?

0–7. Number of days.   9. DK; Refused (coded missing)

DEPENDENT VARIABLES

DIFFUSE SUPPORT MEASURES

I have a few more questions about the institutions of the government in Washington—that is, the Presidency, the Supreme Court, and Congress. In general, do you strongly approve, approve, disapprove, or strongly disapprove of . . .

APPROVE PRESIDENT   The institution of the Presidency, no matter who is in office?

1. Strongly approve   2. Approve   3. Disapprove

4. Strongly disapprove   5. DK; Refused (coded missing)

(Recoded: 1=4, 2=3, 3=2, 4=1)

APPROVE COURT   What about the Supreme Court, no matter who the justices are? [options and recoding as above]

APPROVE CONGRESS   What about the U.S. Congress, no matter who is in office? [options and recoding as above]

APPROVE STRUCTURE   What about the basic constitutional structure of the U.S. government? [options and recoding as above]

DIFFUSE SUPPORT INDEX

The above four variables are combined to form this index.

SPECIFIC SUPPORT

JOB PERFORMANCE MEASURES OF OFFICEHOLDERS   Again, thinking about people in government, please tell me if you strongly approve, approve, disapprove, or strongly disapprove of the way the people are handling their jobs.

JOB COURT   How do you feel about the way the nine justices on the Supreme Court have been handling their job? Do you . . .

1. Strongly approve   2. Approve   3. Disapprove

4. Strongly disapprove   5. DK; Refused (coded missing)

(Recoded: 1=4, 2=3, 3=2, 4=1)

JOB PRESIDENT   What about President George Bush? [options and recoding as above]

JOB CONGRESS   What about the 535 members of Congress? [options and recoding as above]

JOB LEADERS   What about the leaders of Congress? [options and recoding as above]

JOB LOCAL REPRESENTATIVE   What about your own representative in the U.S. House of Representatives? [options and recoding as above]

SPECIFIC SUPPORT—POWER MEASURES

The institutions of government in Washington, no matter who is in office, need a certain amount of power for the good of the country and the individual person. Please tell me if the institution has too much power, not enough power, or about the right amount of power.

POWER COURT The U.S. Supreme Court has too much power, not enough power, or about the right amount of power.

1. Too much power   2. About the right amount of power
3. Not enough power   4. DK; Refused (coded missing)

POWER PRESIDENT   What about the Presidency?

[options and recoding as above]

POWER CONGRESS   What about the U.S. Congress?

[options and recoding as above]

POWER CONGRESS (INVERSE)   Congressional power variable is recoded to align with presidential power component: 3=1, 2=2, 1=3.

SPECIFIC SUPPORT INDEX—PRESIDENT

JOB PRESIDENT, POWER PRESIDENT and POWER CONGRESS (INVERSE) are combined to form this index.

SPECIFIC SUPPORT INDEX—CONGRESS

JOB CONGRESS, JOB LEADERS, LOCAL REPRESENTATIVE and POWER CONGRESS are combined to form this index.

SPECIFIC SUPPORT INDEX—SUPREME COURT

JOB COURT and POWER COURT   are combined to form this index.

APPENDIX C

June 1997 Survey Questions
(Fredericksburg, VA. Area)

Please circle the number next to your choice. Please answer the questions honestly, there are no right or wrong answers. You will not be identified by name in this project. Thank you. For this set of statements, the following coding applies.

1. Agree Strongly

2. Agree Somewhat

3. Neutral — Neither Agree nor Disagree

4. Disagree Somewhat

5. Disagree Strongly

9. Don't Know

We would get better policies from government if more people told their elected officials what they want from them.

1	2	3	4	5	9
AGREE STRONGLY		NEUTRAL		DISAGREE STRONGLY	DON'T KNOW

The American form of government is the best possible.

1	2	3	4	5	9
AGREE STRONGLY		NEUTRAL		DISAGREE STRONGLY	DON'T KNOW

There are times when it is necessary for the government in Washington to bend or even break the law if it is to do its job.

1	2	3	4	5	9

AGREE   NEUTRAL   DISAGREE   DON'T
STRONGLY   STRONGLY   KNOW

We can solve our country's problems without having to make any really big changes in our form of government.

1	2	3	4	5	9

AGREE   NEUTRAL   DISAGREE   DON'T
STRONGLY   STRONGLY   KNOW

Problems such as scandals and corruption in Washington are primarily the fault of individual politicians, not the system.

1	2	3	4	5	9

AGREE   NEUTRAL   DISAGREE   DON'T
STRONGLY   STRONGLY   KNOW

Special interests have too much power now in Washington.

1	2	3	4	5	9

AGREE   NEUTRAL   DISAGREE   DON'T
STRONGLY   STRONGLY   KNOW

People who feel that state governments should have more power and that Washington should have less power are on the right track.

1	2	3	4	5		9
AGREE STRONGLY	NEUTRAL			DISAGREE STRONGLY		DON'T KNOW

My state government has too much power now.

1	2	3	4	5		9
AGREE STRONGLY	NEUTRAL			DISAGREE STRONGLY		DON'T KNOW

Most of the national government's programs over the years have worked out for the good of the country.

1	2	3	4	5		9
AGREE STRONGLY	NEUTRAL			DISAGREE STRONGLY		DON'T KNOW

Most of the state government's programs over the years have worked out for the good of Virginia.

1	2	3	4	5		9
AGREE STRONGLY	NEUTRAL			DISAGREE STRONGLY		DON'T KNOW

Many local elections aren't important enough to bother with.

1	2	3	4	5		9
AGREE STRONGLY	NEUTRAL			DISAGREE STRONGLY		DON'T KNOW

People like me don't have any say about what the government in Washington does.

1	2	3	4	5		9

AGREE   NEUTRAL   DISAGREE   DON'T
STRONGLY   STRONGLY   KNOW

People like me don't have any say about what the government in Richmond does.

1	2	3	4	5		9

AGREE   NEUTRAL   DISAGREE   DON'T
STRONGLY   STRONGLY   KNOW

Sometimes politics and government seem so complicated that a person like me can't understand what's going on.

1	2	3	4	5		9

AGREE   NEUTRAL   DISAGREE   DON'T
STRONGLY   STRONGLY   KNOW

Most people would not try to take advantage of you if they got the chance; instead they would try to be fair.

1	2	3	4	5		9

AGREE   NEUTRAL   DISAGREE   DON'T
STRONGLY   STRONGLY   KNOW

If people were not closely regulated by strong laws, most of them would behave like animals.

| 1 | 2 | 3 | 4 | 5 | 9 |

AGREE   NEUTRAL   DISAGREE   DON'T
STRONGLY   STRONGLY   KNOW

How strong is your love of country: extremely strong, very strong, somewhat strong, or not very strong?

    1. Extremely strong   2. Very strong   3. Somewhat strong
    4. Not very strong   9. Don't know

How strong is your love of Virginia: extremely strong, very strong, somewhat strong, or not very strong?

    1. Extremely strong   2. Very strong   3. Somewhat strong
    4. Not very strong   9. Don't know

Think of the five houses or apartments closest to you on your street or in your building. Each household asks to borrow your TV for an evening when you won't be using it. How many of those households do you trust enough to loan them your TV (or would loan your TV if you had one)?

    0. None   1. One   2. Two   3. Three   4. Four   5. All five
    9. Don't know

Which of the following part or parts of the national government makes you feel most proud? (circle all that apply)

    1. Supreme Court justices   2. President   3. Members of Congress   5. None
    9. Don't know

We find that people differ in how much faith and confidence they have in various levels of government in this country. Do you have more faith and confidence in the national government, the government of this state, or in the local government around here?

     1. National   2. State   3. Local (city and/or county)
     4. None   5. All   9. Don't know

Which level of government do you have the least faith and confidence in?

     1. National   2. State   3. Local (city and/or county)
     4. None   5. All   9. Don't know

Did you vote in the 1996 elections?

     1. Yes
     2. No, but I was old enough to vote in 1996
     3. No, I was not old enough to vote in 1996
     9. Don't Know

Which candidate did you favor for president last November?

     1. Bill Clinton   2. Bob Dole   3. Ross Perot   4. Other
     5. None   9. Don't know

Do you plan to vote in the state elections this fall?

     1. Yes   2. Maybe   3. No

If the election were today, who would you support for governor?

     1. Donald S. Beyer Jr.   2. James S. Gilmore III   3. Other   4. Undecided

Where do you usually get most of your news about what's going on in the world today — is it from the newspapers, radio, television, magazines, or talking with others?

    1. Newspapers   2. Radio   3. Television
    4. Magazines   5. Talking with others   9. Don't know

Your religion is:

    1. Protestant   2. Catholic   3. Jewish   4. Muslim   5. Other/No religion

Do you consider yourself a born-again Christian?

    1. Yes   2. Maybe   3. No

Do you consider yourself a Republican, a Democrat, an Independent, or what?

    1. Republican   2. Democrat   3. Independent
    4. Other (please write in at right) _____
    8. None/Apolitical
    9. Don't Know

In your estimation, your family income makes your family:

    1. Lower or working class   2. Middle class
    3. Upper-middle class   4. Upper class   9. Don't know

We hear a lot of talk these days about liberals and conservatives. Do you consider yourself liberal, slightly liberal, moderate, slightly conservative, or conservative?

    1. Liberal   2. Slightly liberal   3. Moderate
    4. Slightly conservative   5. Conservative   9. Don't know

Are you: 1. Male   2. Female

What is the highest level of school you have completed?
      1. Less than high school   2. Some high school
      3. High school graduate   4. Some technical school
      5. Technical school graduate   6. Some college
      7. College graduate   8. Post graduate or professional degree
      9. Don't know

If you are now in school, where do you attend? _____

What are you studying? _____

What is your current occupation? _____

Are you:

      1. White   2. African American or Black
      3. Latino or Hispanic   4. Asian or Pacific Islander
      5. Native American   6. Other
      9. Don't know

Please write in your age.   _____

Please write in your city and county
and state of birth.   _____

Please write in your city and county
and state of current residence.   _____

Have you ever lived outside Virginia for more than 12 months at a time?

       Yes   No

If so, how old were you when you
were living outside Virginia?   _____

Thank you.

APPENDIX D

June 1997 Fredericksburg, Va. Area Interviewees

This appendix provides information on the survey and interview participants. Participants were informed at the start of the survey that they would be identified by a first name not their own in reports relating to this study.

For education, HS stands for high school, CC stands for community college, C for college/university and G for graduate school. Most/Least refers to the levels of government in which the respondent has the most and least faith.

PV1997 refers to the party of the candidate the respondent prefers for governor of Virginia in the November 1997 election. The Republican candidate is James S. Gilmore III, who had been serving as attorney general; the Democratic candidate is Donald S. Beyer Jr., who had been serving as lieutenant governor. Incumbent GOP Governor George Allen could not run for reelection because of a term limit law.

The interviewees:

Name: Anne.	Name: Bonnie.
Age: 20.	Age: 20.
Race: White.	Race: White.
Education: CC student.	Education: CC student.
Party: None/Apolitical.	Party: None/Apolitical.
Ideology: Slightly liberal.	Ideology: Slightly liberal.
Religion: Other/None.	Religion: Protestant.
Born Again: No.	Born Again: No.
1996 Vote: Dole.	1996 Vote: Clinton.
PV1997: Undecided.	PV1997: R.
Most/Least: National/State.	Most/Least: National/None.

Name: Christopher.

Age: 24.

Race: White.

Education: HS graduate.

Party: None/Apolitical.

Ideology: Don't know.

Religion: Other/None.

Born Again: No.

1996 Vote: Didn't vote.

PV1997: Undecided.

Most/Least: None/National.

Name: Elgin.

Age: 42.

Race: African American.

Education: Some college.

Party: Independent.

Ideology: Slightly liberal.

Religion: Other/None.

Born Again: Yes.

1996 Vote: Clinton.

PV1997: Undecided.

Most/Least: National/Local.

Name: George.

Age: 24.

Race: African American.

Education: Some college.

Party: None/Apolitical.

Ideology: Moderate.

Religion: Protestant.

Born Again: Maybe.

1996 Vote: Perot.

PV1997: Won't vote.

Most/Least: All/State.

Name: Daniel.

Age: 32.

Race: White.

Education: HS graduate.

Party: Don't know.

Ideology: Don't know.

Religion: Jewish.

Born Again: No.

1996 Vote: Didn't vote.

PV1997: Won't vote.

Most/Least: None/National.

Name: Francine.

Age: 23.

Race: White.

Education: College graduate.

Party: Democrat.

Ideology: Liberal.

Religion: Other/None.

Born Again: No.

1996 Vote: Clinton.

PV1997: D.

Most/Least: National/State.

Name: Hannah.

Age: 20.

Race: White.

Education: College student.

Party: Independent.

Ideology: Moderate.

Religion: Protestant.

Born Again: No.

1996 Vote: Other.

PV1997: Undecided.

Most/Least: Don't know/National.

Name: Irene.
Age: 21.
Race: African American.
Education: College student.
Party: Democrat.
Ideology: Slightly liberal.
Religion: Other/None.
Born Again: No.
1996 Vote: Clinton.
PV1997: Undecided.
Most/Least: Local/State.

Name: Kate.
Age: 46.
Race: White.
Education: College gradu-
ate.
Party: Democrat.
Ideology: Slightly liberal.
Religion: Protestant.
Born Again: No.
1996 Vote: Clinton.
PV1997: D.
Most/Least: Local/State.

Name: Martha.
Age: 23.
Race: White.
Education: College gradu-
ate.
Party: Independent.
Religion: Protestant.
Born Again: Yes.
Ideology: Conservative.
1996 Vote: Dole.
PV1997: R.
Most/Least: State/National.

Name: Julie.
Age: 18.
Race: White.
Education: College student.
Party: Independent.
Ideology: Slightly conservative.
Religion: Protestant.
Born Again: No.
1996 Vote: Dole.
PV1997: Undecided.
Most/Least: National/Local.

Name: Laura.
Age: 33.
Race: White.
Education: Some college.

Party: Democrat.
Ideology: Conservative.
Religion: Protestant.
Born Again: No.
1996 Vote: Dole.
PV1997: Undecided.
Most/Least: State/Local.

Name: Nancy.
Age: 27.
Race: African American.
Education: HS graduate.

Party: Independent.
Religion: Baptist (Write-in).
Born Again: Yes.
Ideology: Don't know.
1996 Vote: Didn't vote.
PV1997: Won't vote.
Most/Least: None/Don't know.

Name: Odetta.
Age: 42.
Race: White.
Education: Some college.
Party: Independent.
Ideology: Moderate.
Religion: Baptist (Write-in).
Born Again: Yes.
1996 Vote: Clinton.
PV1997: Undecided.
Most/Least: National/State.

Name: Pauline.
Age: 23.
Race: White.
Education: College graduate.
Party: Independent.
Ideology: Conservative.
Religion: Protestant.
Born Again: Yes.
1996 Vote: Dole.
PV1997: R.
Most/Least: State/National.

Name: Quentin.
Age: 21.
Race: White.
Education: College student.
Party: Libertarian (Write-in).
Ideology: Slightly liberal.
Religion: Protestant.
Born Again: No.
1996 Vote: Clinton.
PV1997: Undecided.
Most/Least: None/National.

Name: Roberta.
Age: 36.
Race: African American.
Education: HS graduate.
Party: Democrat.
Ideology: Moderate.
Religion: Other/None.
Born Again: No.
1996 Vote: Didn't vote.
PV1997: Won't vote.
Most/Least: None/National.

Name: Sarah.
Age: 63.
Race: White.
Education: Some college.
Party: Independent.
Ideology: Slightly conservative.
Religion: Protestant.
Born Again: No.
1996 Vote: Dole.
PV1997: D.
Most/Least State/National.

Name: Theresa.
Age: 25.
Race: White.
Education: Some college.
Party: Republican.
Ideology: Conservative.
Religion: Protestant.
Born Again: Yes.
1996 Vote: Dole.
PV1997: Undecided.
Most/Least: Local/National.

Bibliography

Adams, William C., et al. 1994. "Before and After 'The Day After': The Unexpected Results of a Television Drama." In *Media Power in Politics*, ed. Doris Graber. 3rd ed. Washington D.C.: CQ Press.

Alwin, Duane F., Ronald L. Cohen, and Theodore M. Newcomb. 1991. *Political Attitudes Over the Life Span: The Bennington Women After Fifty Years*. Madison: University of Wisconsin Press.

American National Election Studies. 2000. Ann Arbor: Center for Political Studies, University of Michigan. Inter-University Consortium for Political and Social Research, distributor. (Also used 1996 ANES study and 1952–1992 Cumulative ANES Study [ICPSR CD0010]).

Arnold, R.D. 1990. *The Logic of Congressional Action*. New Haven, Conn.: Yale University Press.

Asher, Herb, and Mike Barr. 1994. "Popular Support for Congress and Its Members." In *Congress, the Press and the Public*, ed. Thomas E. Mann and Norman Ornstein. Washington, D.C.: American Enterprise Institute and Brookings Institution.

Atkeson, Lonna R., and Randall W. Partin. 1995. "Economic and Referendum Voting: A Comparison of Gubernatorial and Senatorial Elections." *American Political Science Review* 89 (March): 99–107.

Atkinson, Frank B. 1992. *The Dynamic Dominion: Realignment and the Rise of Virginia's Republican Party Since 1945*. Fairfax, Va.: George Mason University Press.

Barta, Carolyn. 1993. *Perot and His People: Disrupting the Balance of Political Power*. Fort Worth, Tex.: Summit Group.

Bartels, Larry M. 1993. "Messages received: The Political Impact of Media Exposure." *American Political Science Review* 87 (June): 267–85.

Beck, Paul Allen. 1974. "A Socialization Theory of Partisan Realignment." In *The Politics of Future Citizens*, ed. Richard G. Niemi and Associates. San Francisco, Calif.: Jossey-Bass.

———. 1984. "Young vs. Old in 1984: Generations and Life Stages in Presidential Nomination Politics." *PS: Political Science & Politics* 19 (summer): 515–24.

Becker, Ted. 1993. "Teledemocracy: Gathering Momentum in State and Local Governance." *Spectrum: The Journal of State Government* 66 (spring): 14–9.

Bennett, Linda L.M., and Stephen Earl Bennett. 1990. *Living with Leviathan: Americans Coming to Terms with Big Government*. Lawrence: University of Kansas Press.

Bennett, Stephen Earl, and Eric Rademacher. 1997. "The 'Age of Indifference' Revisited: Patterns of Political Interest, Media Exposure and Knowledge among Generation X." In *After the Boom: The Politics of Generation X*, ed. Stephen C. Craig and Stephen Earl Bennett. Lanham, Md.: Rowman & Littlefield.

Bennett, W. Lance. 2001. *News: The Politics of Illusion*. 4th ed. New York: Addison Wesley Longman.

Berry, Frances Stokes, and William D. Berry. 1992. "Tax Innovation in the States: Capitalizing on Political Opportunity." *American Journal of Political Science* 36 (August): 715–42.

———. 1994. "The Politics of Tax Increases in the States." *American Journal of Political Science* 38 (August): 855–59.

Beyle, Thad. 1993. "Being Governor." In *The State of the States*, ed. Carl E. Van Horn. 2nd ed. Washington, D.C.: CQ Press.

Biskupic, Joan. 1995. "Has the Court Lost Its Appeal? In Poll 59% Can Name 3 'Stooges,' 17% Can Name 3 Justices." *Washington Post*, October 12: A23.

Black, Earl. 1983. "A Theory of Southern Factionalism." *Journal of Politics* 45 (August): 594–614.

Booth, William. 2002. "Economic Anxiety Worries Politicians." *Washington Post*, July 21: A1.

Boyte, Harry C. 1990. "The Growth of Citizen Politics: Stages in Local Community Organizing." *Dissent* 37 (fall): 513–18.

———. 1994. "Populist: Citizenship as Public Work and Public Freedom." In *Building a Community of Citizens: Civil Society and the 21st Century*, ed. Don C. Eberly. Lanham, Md.: University Press of America.

Broder, David S. 2000. *Democracy Derailed: Initiative Campaigns and the Power of Money*. New York: Harcourt.

Bugliosi, Vincent. 2001. *The Betrayal of America: How the Supreme Court Undermined the Constitution and Chose Our President*. New York: Nation Books.

Burns, James MacGregor, et al. 1993. *State and Local Politics: Government by the People*. 7th ed. Englewood Cliffs, N.J.: Prentice-Hall.

Caldeira, Gregory A., and James L. Gibson. 1992. "The Etiology of Public Support for the Supreme Court." *American Journal of Political Science* 36 (August): 635–64.

Cammisa, Anne Marie. 1998. *From Rhetoric to Reform? Welfare Policy in American Politics*. Boulder, Colo.: Westview.

Campbell, Angus, Philip E. Converse, Warren E. Miller, and Donald E. Stokes. 1980. *The American Voter*. Chicago, Ill.: University of Chicago Press. Midway Reprint. Originally published 1960.

Campbell, James E. 1992. "Forecasting the Presidential Vote in the States." *American Journal of Political Science* 36 (May): 386–407.

———. 2001. "The Referendum That Didn't Happen." *PS: Political Science & Politics* 34 (March): 33–38.

Cantril, Hadley. 1940. *The Invasion from Mars: A Study in the Psychology of Panic.* Princeton, N.J.: Princeton University Press.

Cappella, Joseph N., and Kathleen Hall Jamieson. 1997. *Spiral of Cynicism: The Press and the Public Good.* New York: Oxford University Press.

Cardin, Benjamin. 1996. Remarks at the Congressional Policy Development Hearing of the Organization, Study and Review Committee of the Democratic Caucus of the U.S. House of Representatives. Washington, D.C. June 20.

Ceaser, James W., and Andrew E. Busch. 1993. *Upside Down and Inside Out: The 1992 Elections and American Politics.* Lanham, Md.: Rowman & Littlefield.

———. 1997. *Losing To Win: The 1996 Elections and American Politics.* Lanham, Md.: Rowman & Littlefield.

———. 2001. *The Perfect Tie: The True Story of the 2000 Presidential Election.* Lanham, Md.: Rowman & Littlefield.

Chrislip, David D. 1994. "American Renewal: Reconnecting Citizens with Public Life." *National Civic Review* 83 (winter/spring): 25–31.

Citrin, Jack. 1996. "Who's the Boss? Direct Democracy and Popular Control of Government." In *Broken Contract? Changing Relationships between Americans and Their Government*, ed. Stephen C. Craig. Boulder, Colo.: Westview.

Connolly, Ceci. 1997. "Some States Racing To Grasp Baton of Power Passed by High Court." *Washington Post*, June 29: A16.

Cook, David T. 2002. "How Returning Deficits Impacts Main Street." *Christian Science Monitor*, July 19: 2.

Cook, Timothy E. 1985. "The Bear Market in Political Socialization and the Costs of Misunderstood Psychological Theories." *American Political Science Review* 79 (December): 1079–93.

———. 1989. *Making Laws and Making News.* Washington, D.C.: Brookings Institution.

———. 1998. *Governing with the News: The News Media as a Political Institution.* Chicago, Ill.: University of Chicago Press.

Corrado, Anthony. 1994. "The 1992 Presidential Election: A time for a Change?" In *The Parties Respond: Changes in American Parties and Campaigns*, ed. L. Sandy Maisel. 2nd ed. Boulder, Colo.: Westview.

Craig, Stephen C. 1993. *The Malevolent Leaders.* Boulder, Colo.: Westview.

———. 1996. "The Angry Voter: Politics and Popular Discontent in the 1990s." In *Broken Contract? Changing Relationships between Americans and Their Government*, ed. Stephen C. Craig. Boulder, Colo.: Westview.

Craig, Stephen C., and Stephen Earl Bennett, eds. 1997. *After the Boom: The Politics of Generation X.* Lanham, Md.: Rowman & Littlefield.

Craig, Stephen C., and Kenneth D. Wald. 1985. "Whose Ox To Gore? A Comment on the Relationship between Political Discontent and Political Violence." *Western Political Quarterly* 38: 652–62.

Cronin, Thomas E. 1989. *Direct Democracy: The Politics of Initiative, Referendum, and Recall.* Cambridge, Mass.: Harvard University Press.

Cronin, Thomas E., and Michael A. Genovese. 1998. "President Clinton and Character Questions." *Presidential Studies Quarterly* 28 (4): 892–97.

Dabney, Virginius. 1971. *Virginia: The New Dominion.* New York: Doubleday.

Dahl, Robert A. 1992. "The Problem of Civic Competence." *Journal of Democracy* 3 (October): 45–59.

Davis, Richard. 1994. *Decisions and Images: The Supreme Court and the Press*. Englewood Cliffs, N.J.: Prentice Hall.

———. 1999. *The Web of Politics*. New York: Oxford University Press.

Davis, Richard, and Diana Owen. 1998. *New Media and American Politics*. New York: Oxford University Press.

Dawson, Richard E., and Kenneth Prewitt. 1969. *Political Socialization*. Boston, Mass.: Little, Brown & Co.

Delli Carpini, Michael X. 1986. *Stability and Change in American Politics: The Coming of Age of the Generation of the 1960s*. New York: New York University Press.

Dennis, Jack. 1970. "Support for the Institution of Elections by the Mass Public." *American Political Science Review* 64 (September): 819–35.

———. 1973. "Major Problems of Political Socialization Research." In *Socialization to Politics: A Reader*, ed. Jack Dennis. New York: John Wiley & Sons.

———. 1976. "Who Supports the Presidency?" *Society* 13 (July/August): 48–53.

———. 1981. "Public Support for Congress." *Political Behavior* 3: 319–50.

Dennis, Jack, and Diana Owen. 1994. "Perot and the Media." Paper presented at the annual meeting of the Midwest Political Science Association, Chicago, Ill., April.

———. 1997. "The Partisanship Puzzle: Identification and Attitudes of Generation X." In *After the Boom: The Politics of Generation X*, ed. Stephen C. Craig and Stephen Earl Bennett. Lanham, Md.: Rowman & Littlefield.

Derthick, Martha. 1987. "American Federalism: Madison's Middle Ground in the 1980s." *Public Administration Review* 47 (January/February): 66–74.

Dionne, E.J., Jr. 1991. *Why Americans Hate Politics*. New York: Simon & Schuster.

Dodd, Lawrence C. 1993. "Congress and the Politics of Renewal: Redressing the Crisis of Legitimation." In *Congress Reconsidered*, ed., Lawrence C. Dodd and Bruce I. Oppenheimer. 5th ed. Washington, D.C.: CQ Press.

Donahue, John D. 1997. "The Disunited States." *The Atlantic Monthly* 279 (May): 18–22.

Downs, Anthony. 1957. *An Economic Theory of Democracy*. New York: Harper & Row.

Drew, Elizabeth. 2002. *Citizen McCain*. New York: Simon & Schuster.

Drudge, Matt. 2000. *Drudge Manifesto*. New York: New American Library.

Durr, Robert H., John B. Gilmour, and Christina Wolbrecht. 1997. "Explaining Congressional Approval." *American Journal of Political Science* 41 (January): 175–204.

Easton, David. 1953. *The Political System: An Inquiry into the State of Political Science*. New York: Alfred A. Knopf.

———. 1965a. *A Framework for Political Analysis*. Englewood Cliffs, N.J.: Prentice-Hall.

———. 1965b. *A Systems Analysis of Political Life*. New York: John Wiley & Sons.

———. 1975. "A Reassessment of the Concept of Political Support." *British Journal of Political Science* 5: 435–57.

———. 1976. "Theoretical Approaches to Political Support." *Canadian Journal of Political Science* 9: 431–48.

———. 1990. *The Analysis of Political Structure*. New York: Routledge.

Easton, David, and Jack Dennis. 1967. "The Child's Acquisition of Regime Norms: Political Efficacy." *American Political Science Review* 61 (March): 25–38.

———. 1969. *Children in the Political System: Origins of Political Legitimacy*. New York: McGraw-Hill.

Edds, Margaret. 1990. *Claiming the Dream: The Victorious Campaign of Douglas Wilder of Virginia*. Chapel Hill, N.C.: Algonquin Books.

Edelman, Murray. 1985. *The Symbolic Uses of Politics*. Urbana-Champaign: University of Illinois Press.

Edsall, Thomas B. 2002. "FEC Rules on 'Issue Ads' Decried." *Washington Post*, August 1: A25.

Edwards, George C., III. 2000. "Campaigning Is Not Governing: Bill Clinton's Rhetorical Presidency." In *The Clinton Legacy*, ed. Colin Campbell and Bert A. Rockman. New York: Chatham House.

Elazar, Daniel. 1972. *American Federalism: A View from the States*. 2nd ed. New York: Crowell.

———. 1976. *The Generational Rhythm of American Politics*. Philadelphia, Pa.: Center for the Study of Federalism, Temple University.

Erikson, Robert S., Michael B. MacKuen, and James A. Stimson. 2001. "Macropartisanship: The Permanent Memory of Partisan Evaluation." In *Controversies in Voting Behavior*, ed. Richard G. Niemi and Herbert F. Weisberg. 4th ed. Washington, D.C.: CQ Press.

Erikson, Robert S., Gerald C. Wright, and John P. McIver. 1993. *Statehouse Democracy: Public Opinion and Policy in the American States*. New York: Cambridge University Press.

Fainaru, Steve, and Dan Eggen. 2002. "Judge Rules U.S. Must Release Detainees' Names." *Washington Post*, August 3: A1.

Farnsworth, Stephen J. 1997. "Political Support in a Frustrated America." Ph.D. diss. Georgetown University.

———. 1999a. "Loving and Loathing Virginia: Feelings about Federalism in the Old Dominion." *Virginia Social Science Journal* 34: 15–38.

———. 1999b. "Federal Frustration, State Satisfaction? Voters and Decentralized Government Power." *Publius: The Journal of Federalism* 29 (3): 75–88.

———. 2000. "Political Support and Citizen Frustration: Testing Three Linkage Theories." *Virginia Social Science Journal* 35: 69–84.

———. 2001a. "Competing Citizen Views of Trust: Virginia Interviews on the Forms of Political and Personal Trust." *Virginia Social Science Journal* 36: 43–59.

———. 2001b. "Patterns of Political Support: Examining Congress and the Presidency." *Congress & the Presidency* 28 (1): 45–61.

———. 2002. "Campaigning against Government in the Old Dominion: State Taxation, State Power and Virginia's 1997 Gubernatorial Election." *Politics & Policy* 30 (3): 460–80.

———. 2003a. "Congress and Citizen Discontent: Public Evaluations of the Membership and One's Own Representative." *American Politics Research* 31 (1): 66–80.

Farnsworth, Stephen J. 2003b. "Citizen Evaluations of the Federal Government." *Virginia Social Science Journal* 38: 1–16.

Farnsworth, Stephen J., and S. Robert Lichter. 2003. *The Nightly News Nightmare: Network Television's Coverage of U.S. Presidential Elections, 1988–2000.* Lanham, Md.: Rowman & Littlefield.

Farnsworth, Stephen J., and Diana M. Owen. 2001. "The Revolution That Wasn't: The Internet and the 2000 Elections." Paper presented at the Annual Meeting of the Southern Political Science Association, Atlanta, Ga., November.

Fenno, Richard F., Jr. 1975. "If, As Ralph Nader Says, Congress Is 'The Broken Branch,' How Come We Love Our Congressmen So Much?" In *Congress and Change: Evolution and Reform*, ed. Norman J. Ornstein. New York: Praeger.

———. 1992. *When Incumbency Fails: The Senate Career of Mark Andrews.* Washington, D.C.: CQ Press.

Fickett, Lewis P. 1985. *American Politics in an Age of Failure: 1963–1985.* Bristol, Ind.: Wyndham Hall Press.

Fiorina, Morris P. 1992. *Divided Government.* New York: Macmillan.

Gallup Organization. 2002. "Bush Approval Drops Below 80% Level." *Gallup Poll News Service.* Poll Analyses, March 8. Available at <http://www.gallup.com>.

Georges, Christopher. 1993. "Perot and Con: Ross's Teledemocracy Is Supposed To Bypass Special Interests and Take the Money out of Politics; It Won't." *Washington Monthly* 25 (June): 38–43.

Gibson, James L., and Gregory A. Caldeira. 1992. "Blacks and the United States Supreme Court: Models of Diffuse Support." *Journal of Politics* 54 (November): 1120–45.

Gingrich, Newt. 1995. *To Renew America.* New York: HarperCollins.

Ginsberg, Benjamin. 1986. *The Captive Public: How Mass Opinion Promotes State Power.* New York: Basic Books.

Gitlin, Todd. 1980. *The Whole World is Watching: Mass Media in the Making and Unmaking of the New Left.* Berkeley: University of California Press.

Glod, Maria. 2002. "Three Slain Girls' Cases Closed." *Washington Post*, August 14: B1.

Gottlieb, Gidon. 1993. *Nation against State: A New Approach to Ethnic Conflicts and the Decline of Sovereignty.* New York: Council on Foreign Relations Press.

Graber, Doris. 1988. *Processing the News*, 2nd ed. New York: Longman.

———. 2002. *Mass Media and American Politics*, 6th ed. Washington, D.C.: CQ Press.

Greider, William. 1992. *Who Will Tell The People: The Betrayal of American Democracy.* New York: Simon & Schuster.

Grossman, Lawrence K. 1995. *The Electronic Republic: Reshaping Democracy in the Information Age.* New York: Penguin.

Gugliotta, Guy. 1995. "Scaling Down the American Dream." *Washington Post*, April 19: A21.

Habermas, Jurgen. 1973. *Legitimation Crisis.* Trans. Thomas McCarthy. Boston, Mass.: Beacon Press.

Halberstam, David. 1979. *The Powers that Be.* New York: Alfred A. Knopf.

Hall, Jim. 2001. *Online Journalism: A Critical Primer.* London, U.K.: Pluto.

Hallin, Daniel C. 1984. "The Media, the War in Vietnam, and Political Support: A Critique of the Thesis of an Oppositional Media." *Journal of Politics* 46 (February): 2–24.

Hamilton, Alexander, James Madison, and John Jay. 1990. *The Federalist*. Ed. George W. Carey and James McClellan. Dubuque, Iowa: Kendall-Hunt. Originally published 1787–1788.

Harris, Richard A. 1997. "The Era of Big Government Lives." *Polity* 30 (fall): 187–92.

Hart, Roderick P. 1994. *Seducing America: How Television Charms the Modern Voter*. New York: Oxford University Press.

Harwood Group. 1991. *Citizens and Politics: A View from Main Street America*. Dayton, Ohio: Kettering Foundation.

Held, David. 1987. *Models of Democracy*. Stanford, Calif.: Stanford University Press.

Herbers, John. 1987. "The New Federalism: Unplanned, Innovative and Here To Stay." *Governing* 1 (October): 28–37.

Hershey, Marjorie Randon. 1997. "The Congressional Elections." In *The Elections of 1996: Reports and Interpretations*, ed. Gerald M. Pomper. Chatham, N.J.: Chatham House.

Hess, Robert D., and Judith V. Torney. 1967. *The Development of Political Attitudes in Children*. Garden City, N.Y.: Anchor Books.

Hetherington, Marc J., and John D. Nugent. 1998. "Explaining Public Support for Devolution: The Role of Political Trust." Paper presented at the Hendricks Symposium on Public Disaffection with the U.S. Political System, Lincoln, Nebr., October.

Hibbing, John R., and Elizabeth Theiss-Morse. 1995. *Congress as Public Enemy: Public Attitudes toward American Political Institutions*. Cambridge, U.K.: Cambridge University Press.

———. 1998. "The Media's Role in Public Negativity toward Congress: Distinguishing Emotional Reactions and Cognitive Evaluations." *American Journal of Political Science* 42 (April): 475–98.

Hill, Kim Quaile. 1994. *Democracy in the Fifty States*. Lincoln: University of Nebraska Press.

Hill, Kim Quaile, Jan E. Leighley, and Angela Hinton-Andersson. 1995. "Lower Class Mobilization and Policy Linkage in the U.S. States." *American Journal of Political Science* 39 (February): 75–86.

Horowitz, Donald L. 1977. *The Courts and Social Policy*. Washington, D.C.: Brookings Institution.

Howe, Neil, and Bill Strauss. 1993. *13th Gen: Abort, Retry, Ignore, Fail?* New York: Vintage.

Hunt, Albert. 1981. "The Campaign and the Issues." In *The American Elections of 1980*, ed. Austin Ranney. Washington, D.C.: American Enterprise Institute.

Huntington, Samuel P. 1981. *American Politics and the Promise of Disharmony*. Cambridge, Mass.: Harvard University Press.

Inglehart, Ronald. 1977. *The Silent Revolution*. Princeton, N.J.: Princeton University Press.

———. 1981. "Post-Materialism in an Environment of Insecurity." *American Political Science Review* 75 (December): 880–900.

———. 1988. "The Renaissance of Political Culture." *American Political Science Review* 82 (December): 1203–30.

———. 1990. *Culture Shift in Advanced Industrial Society*. Princeton, N.J.: Princeton University Press.

Iyengar, Shanto. 1991. *Is Anyone Responsible? How Television Frames Political Issues*. Chicago, Ill.: University of Chicago Press.

Iyengar, Shanto, and Donald R. Kinder. 1987. *News That Matters*. Chicago, Ill.: University of Chicago Press.

Jackson, Brooks. 1997. "Financing the 1996 Campaign: The Law of the Jungle." In *Toward the Millennium: The Elections of 1996*, ed. Larry J. Sabato. Boston, Mass.: Allyn and Bacon.

Jackson, John S., III, and William Crotty. 2001. *The Politics of Presidential Selection*, 2nd ed. New York: Longman.

Jacobson, Gary C. 2001. *The Politics of Congressional Elections*, 5th ed. New York: Longman.

Jaros, Dean, and Robert Roper. 1980. "The U.S. Supreme Court: Myth, Diffuse Support, Specific Support and Political Legitimacy." *American Politics Quarterly* 8: 85–105.

Jennings, M. Kent, and Richard G. Niemi. 1968. "The Transmission of Political Values from Parent to Child." *American Political Science Review* 62 (March): 169–84.

———. 1974. *The Political Character of Adolescence*. Princeton, N.J.: Princeton University Press.

———. 1981. *Generations and Politics: A Panel Study of Young Adults and Their Parents*. Princeton, N.J.: Princeton University Press.

Jewell, Malcolm. 1982. *Representation in State Legislatures*. Lexington: University of Kentucky Press.

Jones, Charles O. 1994. *The Presidency in a Separated System*. Washington, D.C.: Brookings Institution.

———. 1995. *Separate but Equal Branches: Congress and the Presidency*. Chatham, N.J.: Chatham House.

Kaase, Max, and Kenneth Newton. 1995. *Beliefs in Government*. Oxford, U.K.: Oxford University Press.

Keeter, Scott. 1997. "Public Opinion and the Election." In *The Elections of 1996: Reports and Interpretations*, ed. Gerald M. Pomper. Chatham, N.J.: Chatham House.

Kerbel, Matthew R. 1995. *Remote and Controlled: Media Politics in a Cynical Age*. Boulder, Colo.: Westview.

———. 1998. *Edited for Television: CNN, ABC and American Presidential Elections*. Boulder, Colo.: Westview.

Key, V.O. 1949. *Southern Politics in State and Nation*. New York: Alfred A. Knopf.

Kimball, David C., and Samuel C. Patterson. 1997. "Living Up to Expectations: Public Attitudes towards Congress." *Journal of Politics* 59 (3): 701–28.

Kinder, Donald R., and David O. Sears. 1985. "Public Opinion and Political Action." In *Handbook of Social Psychology*, ed. Gardner Lindzey and Elliot Aronson. 3rd ed. New York: Random House.

Klain, Ronald A., and Jeremy B. Bash. 2002. "The Labor of Sisyphus: The Gore

Recount Perspective." In *Overtime! The Election 2000 Thriller*, ed. Larry J. Sabato. New York: Longman.

Klapper, Joseph. 1960. *The Effects of Mass Media*. Glencoe, Ill.: Free Press.

Kohut, Andrew. 2002. "Increasingly It's the Economy that Scares Us." *New York Times*, July 14: Section 4, p. 15.

Krickus, Richard J. 1987. *The Superpowers in Crisis: Implications of Domestic Discord*. McLean, Va.: Pergamon-Brassey's.

Kunde, James E. 1994. "American Renewal: The Challenge of Leadership." *National Civic Review* 83 (winter/spring): 17–24.

Kurtz, Howard. 2002. "Troubled Times for Network Evening News." *Washington Post*, March 10: A1.

Kushma, John J. 1988. "Participation and the Democratic Agenda: Theory and Praxis." In *The State and Democracy: Revitalizing America's Government*, ed. Marc V. Levine, et al. New York: Routledge, Chapman & Hall.

Lane, Charles. 2002. "U.S. Court Votes To Bar Pledge of Allegiance; Use of 'God' Called Unconstitutional." *Washington Post*, June 27: A1.

Lane, Robert E. 1962. *Political Ideology: Why the American Common Man Believes as He Does*. New York: Free Press.

Lascher, Edward L., Jr., Michael Hagen, and Steven A. Rochlin. 1996. "Gun Behind the Door? Ballot Initiatives, State Politics and Public Opinion." *Journal of Politics* 58 (August): 760–75.

Lazare, Daniel. 1996. *The Frozen Republic: How the Constitution Is Paralyzing Democracy*. New York: Harcourt Brace.

Lazarsfeld, Paul F., Bernard Berelson, and Hazel Gaudet. 1948. *The People's Choice*. New York: Columbia University Press.

Lesher, Stephan. 1982. *Media Unbound: The Impact of Television Journalism on the Public*. Boston, Mass.: Houghton-Mifflin.

Lewis-Beck, Michael S., and Tom W. Rice. 1992. *Forecasting Elections*. Washington, D.C.: CQ Press.

Lippmann, Walter. 1965. *Public Opinion*. New York: Free Press. Originally published 1922.

Lowi, Theodore J. 1979. *The End of Liberalism: The Second Republic of the United States*, 2nd ed. New York: W.W. Norton & Co.

———. 1985. *The Personal President: Power Invested, Promise Unfilled*. Ithaca, N.Y.: Cornell University Press.

Magleby, David B. 1984. *Direct Legislation: Voting on Ballot Propositions in the United States*. Baltimore, Md.: Johns Hopkins University Press.

Mann, Thomas E. 1996. Remarks at the Congressional Policy Development Hearing of the Organization, Study and Review Committee of the Democratic Caucus of the U.S. House of Representatives. Washington, D.C. June 20.

Mann, Thomas E., and Norman J. Ornstein, eds. 1995. *Intensive Care: How Congress Shapes Health Policy*. Washington, D.C.: American Enterprise Institute and Brookings Institution.

Mannheim, Karl. 1952. "The Problem of Generations." In *Essays on the Sociology of Knowledge*, ed. Paul Kecskemeti. London: Routledge & Kegan Paul.

Mason, David S. 1995. "Justice, Socialism and Participation in the Post-Communist States." In *Social Justice and Political Change: Public Opinion in*

Capitalist and Post-Communist States, ed., James R. Kluegel, David S. Mason and Bernd Wegener. Hawthorne, N.Y.: Aldine De Gruyter.

Matthews, David. 1994. *Politics for People: Finding a Responsible Public Voice*. Chicago: University of Illinois Press.

Mayer, Jane, and Jill Abramson. 1994. *Strange Justice: The Selling of Clarence Thomas*. Boston, Mass.: Houghton Mifflin.

Mayer, Kenneth R., and David T. Canon. 1999. *The Dysfunctional Congress? The Individual Roots of an Institutional Dilemma*. Boulder, Colo.: Westview.

Mayhew, David R. 1974. *Congress: The Electoral Connection*. New Haven, Conn.: Yale University Press.

———. 1991. *Divided We Govern*. New Haven, Conn.: Yale University Press.

McCombs, Maxwell E., and Donald L. Shaw. 1977. *The Emergence of American Political Issues: The Agenda-Setting Function of the Press*. St. Paul, Minn.: West Publishing Co.

McGinniss, Joe. 1969. *The Selling of a President 1968*. New York: Trident Press.

Merida, Kevin, and Michael A. Fletcher. 2002. "Supreme Discomfort." *Washington Post Magazine*, August 4: W8.

Meyrowitz, Joshua. 1985. *No Sense of Place: The Impact of Electronic Media on Social Behavior*. New York: Oxford University Press.

Miller, Warren E. 1992. "Generational Changes and Party Identification." *Political Behavior* 14 (September): 333–60.

Miller, Warren E., Donald R. Kinder, Steven J. Rosenstone, and the American National Election Studies. 1994. *American National Election Studies: Cumulative Surveys: 1952–1992*. (computer file.) Ann Arbor: Center for Political Studies, University of Michigan: distributed by Inter-university Consortium for Political and Social Research.

Nathan, Richard P. 1990. "Federalism: The Great 'Composition.' " In *The New American Political System*, ed. Anthony King. 2nd version. Washington, D.C.: AEI Press.

Nelson, Michael. 1997. "The Election: Turbulence and Tranquility in Contemporary American Politics." In *The Elections of 1996*, ed. Michael Nelson. Washington, D.C.: CQ Press.

Neuman, W. Russell. 1986. *The Paradox of Mass Politics: Knowledge and Opinion in the American Electorate*. Cambridge, Mass.: Harvard University Press.

Neustadt, Richard E. 1990. *Presidential Power and the Modern Presidents*. New York: Free Press.

Nie, Norman H., Sidney Verba, and John R. Petrocik. 1979. *The Changing American Voter*. Cambridge, Mass.: Harvard University Press.

Niemi, Richard G., Harold W. Stanley, and Richard J. Vogel. 1995. "State Economies and State Taxes: Do Voters Hold Governors Accountable?" *American Journal of Political Science* 39 (November): 936–57.

Nimmo, Dan, and James E. Combs. 1980. *Subliminal Politics*. Englewood Cliffs, N.J.: Prentice-Hall.

Nincic, Miroslav. 1997. "Loss Aversion and the Domestic Context of Military Intervention." *Political Research Quarterly* 50 (1): 97–120.

Norris, Pippa. 2000. *A Virtuous Circle: Political Communication in Post-Industrial Societies*. New York: Cambridge University Press.

O'Brien, David M. 2000. *Storm Center: The Supreme Court in American Politics*, 5th ed. New York: W.W. Norton.

Offe, Claus. 1984. *Contradictions of the Welfare State*. Cambridge, Mass.: MIT Press.

Olsen, Marvin E. 1982. *Participatory Pluralism: Political Participation and Influence in the United States and Sweden*. Chicago, Ill.: Nelson-Hall.

Owen, Diana. 1991. *Media Messages in American Presidential Elections*. New York: Greenwood Press.

———. 1996. "Who's Talking? Who's Listening? The New Politics of Talk Radio Shows." In *Broken Contract? Changing Relationships between Americans and Their Government*, ed. Stephen C. Craig. Boulder, Colo.: Westview.

———. 2000. "Popular Politics and the Clinton/Lewinsky Affair: The Implications for Leadership." *Political Psychology* 21 (1): 161–77.

Owen, Diana, and Jack Dennis. 1990. "Communication Influences upon Institutional Political Socialization." Paper presented at the annual scientific meeting of the International Society of Political Psychology, Washington, D.C., July.

———. 1994. "The Political Origins of the Grunge Generation: The Development of Partisan Orientations." Paper presented at the annual meeting of the American Association for Public Opinion Research, Danvers, Mass., May.

———. 1996. "Anti-Partyism in the USA and Support for Ross Perot." *European Journal of Political Research* 29 (April): 383–400.

Owen, Diana, and Stephen J. Farnsworth. 1995. "Public Support for Electronic Town Meetings." Paper presented at the annual meeting of the Southern Political Science Association, Tampa, Fla., November.

Page, Benjamin I., and Robert Y. Shapiro. 1992. *The Rational Public: Fifty Years of Trends in American Policy Preferences*. Chicago, Ill.: University of Chicago Press.

Parker, Suzanne Lee. 1986. "The Dynamics of Changing System Support in the United States: 1964–1980." Ph.D. diss., Florida State University.

Patterson, Samuel C. 1996. "Legislative Politics in the States." In *Politics in the American States: A Comparative Perspective*, ed. Virginia Gray and Herbert Jacobs. 6th ed. Washington, D.C.: CQ Press.

Patterson, Thomas E. 1980. *The Mass Media Election: How Americans Choose Their President*. New York: Praeger.

———. 1993. *Out of Order*. New York: Alfred A. Knopf.

Perret, Geoffrey. 2001. *Jack: A Life Like No Other*. New York: Random House.

Pew Research Center for the People and the Press. 2000a. "Media Seen as Fair, But Tilting to Gore." Survey Reports October 15. Available at <http://www.people-press.org>.

———. 2000b. "Internet Elections News Audience Seeks Convenience, Familiar Names." Survey Reports, December 3. Available at <http://www.people-press.org>.

Pierre, Robert E. 2002. "Fear and Anxiety Permeate Arab Enclave Near Detroit." *Washington Post*, August 4: A3.

Poggi, Gianfranco. 1990. *The State: Its Nature, Development and Prospects*. Cambridge, U.K.: Polity Press.

Popkin, Samuel. 1991. *The Reasoning Voter*. Chicago, Ill.: University of Chicago Press.

Postman, Neil. 1985. *Amusing Ourselves to Death: Public Discourse in the Age of Show Business*. New York: Penguin.

Priest, Dana, and Helen Dewar. 2002. "Security Agency Led FBI to Capitol Hill." *Washington Post*, August 3: A2.

Putnam, Robert D. 1973. *The Beliefs of Politicians: Ideology, Conflict and Democracy in Britain and Italy*. New Haven, Conn.: Yale University Press.

———. 1993a. *Making Democracy Work*. Princeton, N.J.: Princeton University Press.

———. 1993b. "What Makes Democracy Work?" *National Civic Review* 82 (spring): 101–7.

———. 1993c. "The Prosperous Community: Social Capital and Economic Growth." *The American Prospect* 1.3 (spring): 35–42.

———. 1995a. "Bowling Alone: America's Declining Social Capital." *Journal of Democracy* 6 (January): 65–78.

———. 1995b. "Tuning in, Tuning out: The Strange Disappearance of Social Capital in America." *PS: Political Science & Politics* 28 (*December*): 664–83.

———. 2000. *Bowling Alone: The Collapse and Revival of American Community*. New York: Simon & Schuster.

Quirk, Paul J., and William Cunion. 2000. "Clinton's Domestic Policy: The Lessons of a 'New Democrat.'" In *The Clinton Legacy*, ed. Colin Campbell and Bert A. Rockman. New York: Chatham House.

Ranney, Austin. 1962. *The Doctrine of Responsible Party Government*. Urbana: University of Illinois Press.

———. 1983. *Channels of Power*. New York: Basic Books.

Rice, Tom W., and Alexander F. Sumberg. 1997. "Civic Culture and Government Performance in the American States." *Publius: The Journal of Federalism* 27 (winter): 99–114.

Rivlin, Alice. 1992. *Reviving the American Dream: The Economy, the States and the Federal Government*. Washington, D.C.: Brookings Institution.

Robinson, Michael J. 1976. "Public Affairs Television and the Growth of Political Malaise: The Case of Selling the Pentagon." *American Political Science Review* 70 (June): 409–32.

———. 1981. "Three Faces of Congressional Media." In *The New Congress*, ed. Thomas E. Mann and Norman J. Ornstein. Washington, D.C.: American Enterprise Institute.

Robinson, Michael J., and Margaret A. Sheehan. 1983. *Over the Wire and on TV: CBS and UPI in Campaign '80*. New York: Russell Sage Foundation.

Roeder, Philip W. 1994. *Public Opinion and Policy Leadership in the American States*. Tuscaloosa: University of Alabama Press.

Rosenau, James N. 1988. "The State in an Era of Cascading Politics: Wavering Concept, Widening Competence, Withering Colossus, or Weathering Change?" *Comparative Political Studies* 21 (April): 13–44.

Rozell, Mark, and Clyde Wilcox. 1996. *A Second Coming: The New Christian Right in Virginia Politics*. Baltimore, Md.: Johns Hopkins University Press.

Rushefsky, Mark E. 1996. *Public Policy in the United States: Toward the 21st Century*. Belmont, Calif.: Wadsworth Publishing Co.

Sabato, Larry J. 1993. *Feeding Frenzy: How Attack Journalism Has Transformed American Politics*. New York: Free Press.

Sabato, Larry J., Mark Stencel, and S. Robert Lichter. 2000. *Peepshow: Media and Politics in an Age of Scandal*. Lanham, Md.: Rowman & Littlefield.

Sapiro, Virginia, and David T. Canon. 2000. "Race, Gender, and the Clinton Presidency." In *The Clinton Legacy*, ed. Colin Campbell and Bert A. Rockman. New York: Chatham House.

Schattschneider, E.E. 1977. *Party Government*. Westport, Conn.: Greenwood Press. Originally published 1942.

Schneider, William. 1981. "The November 4 Vote for President: What Did it Mean?" In *The American Elections of 1980*, ed. Austin Ranney. Washington, D.C.: American Enterprise Institute.

Sears, David O., Tom R. Tyler, Jack Citrin, and Donald R. Kinder. 1978. "Political System Support and Public Response to the Energy Crisis." *American Journal of Political Science* 22 (February): 56–82.

Seib, Philip. 2001. *Going Live: Getting the News Right in a Real-Time Online World*. Lanham, Md.: Rowman & Littlefield.

Skocpol, Theda. 1997. *Boomerang: Health Care Reform and the Turn against Government*. New York: W.W. Norton & Co.

Sniderman, Paul M. 1981. *A Question of Loyalty*. Berkeley: University of California Press.

Squire, Peverill. 1993. "Professionalism and Public Opinion of State Legislatures." *Journal of Politics* 55 (May): 478–91.

Stevenson, Richard W. 2002. "White House Says It Expects Deficit To Hit $165 Billion." *New York Times*, July 12: A1.

Stevenson, Richard W., and Janet Elder. 2002. "Poll Finds Concerns that Bush Is Overly Influenced by Business." *New York Times*, July 18: A1.

Stewart, Marianne C. 1986. "A State of Heart, A State of Mind: Political Support in Canada." Ph.D. diss., Duke University.

Strauss, William, and Neil Howe. 1991. *Generations: The History of America's Future, 1584 to 2069*. New York: Morrow.

Sunstein, Cass. 2001. *Republic.com*. Princeton, N.J.: Princeton University Press.

Tapper, Jake. 2001. *Down and Dirty: The Plot To Steal the Presidency*. Boston: Little, Brown.

———. 2002. "*Down and Dirty*, Revisited: A Postscript on Florida and the News Media." In *Overtime! The Election 2000 Thriller*, ed. Larry J. Sabato. New York: Longman.

Terwilliger, George W. 2002. "The Campout for Lawyers: The Bush Recount Perspective." In *Overtime! The Election 2000 Thriller*, ed. Larry J. Sabato. New York: Longman.

Tocqueville, Alexis de. 1960. *Democracy in America*. New York: Vintage Books. Originally published 1835.

Tolchin, Susan J. 1999. *The Angry American: How Voter Rage Is Changing the Nation*, 2nd ed. Boulder, Colo.: Westview.

Turner, Frederick Jackson. 1962. *The Frontier in American History*. New York: Holt, Rinehart and Winston.

Tyler, Tom R. 1988. "What is Procedural Justice?" *Law & Society Review* 22 (1): 103–35.

Tyler, Tom R., and Kenneth A. Rasinksi. 1991. "Procedural Justice, Institutional

Legitimacy and the Acceptance of Unpopular U.S. Supreme Court Decisions: A Reply to Gibson." *Law & Society Review* 25 (3): 621–30.

U.S. Bureau of the Census. 1997. *Statistical Abstract of the United States.* 117th ed. Washington, D.C.: Author.

Vig, Norman J., and Michael E. Kraft. 2003. *Environmental Policy: New Directions for the Twenty-First Century,* 5th ed. Washington, D.C.: CQ Press.

Waterman, Richard W., Robert Wright, and Gilbert St. Clair. 1999. *The Image-Is-Everything Presidency.* Boulder, Colo.: Westview.

Wayne, Stephen J. 2003. *Is This Any Way To Run a Democratic Election?* Boston, Mass.: Houghton Mifflin.

Weatherford, M. Stephen. 1987. "How Does Government Performance Influence Political Support?" *Political Behavior* 9 (1): 5–28.

Weisman, Jonathan. 2002. "Remember Fiscal Discipline?" *Washington Post,* August 9: A1.

Wertheimer, Fred. 2002. "Soft Money's Big Comeback." *Washington Post,* August 2: A23.

Wetstein, Matthew E., and Robert B. Albritton. 1995. "Effects of Public Opinion on Abortion Policies and Use in the American States." *Publius: The Journal of Federalism* 25 (Fall): 91–105.

White, Theodore H. 1961. *The Making of the President 1960.* New York: Atheneum House.

———. 1978. *In Search of History.* New York: Warner Books.

Wilkinson, J. Harvie, III. 1968. *Harry Byrd and the Changing Face of Virginia Politics 1945–66.* Charlottesville: University of Virginia Press.

Wilson, Woodrow. 1908. *Constitutional Government in the United States.* New York: Columbia University Press.

Wlezien, Christopher. 2001. "On Forecasting the Presidential Vote." *PS: Political Science & Politics* 34 (March): 25–31.

Wood, Christopher A. 1995. "The War for Western Lands." *Washington Post,* May 7: C2.

Woodward, Bob. 1999. *Shadow: Five Presidents and the Legacy of Watergate.* New York: Simon & Schuster.

Wright, James D. 1976. *The Dissent of the Governed: Alienation and Democracy in America.* New York: Academic Press.

Yankelovich, Daniel. 1991. *Coming to Public Judgment: Making Democracy Work in a Complex World.* Syracuse, N.Y.: Syracuse University Press.

Index

About the Author

STEPHEN J. FARNSWORTH is associate professor of political science and international affairs at Mary Washington College in Fredericksburg, VA, and co-author of *The Nightly News Nightmare: Network Television's Coverage of U.S. Presidential Elections, 1988–2000* (2003).